EMBRACE YOUR CROWN

OPEN 5 GATES TO OVERCOME UNBELIEF

YOUR BIGGEST
THREAT TO PROGRESS
IS UNBELIEF

Copyright © 2024 K. Lee

Published by Krystal Lee Enterprises LLC (KLE Publishing)
All rights reserved. No parts of this book may be reproduced, distributed, or used in any manner, including photocopying, recording, or other electronic or mechanical methods without the prior written permission of the copywriter owner, except for the use of brief quotations in a book review and certain noncommercial uses permitted by copyright law.

ISBN: 978-1-945066-65-8

Paperback:
All rights reserved. Please send comments and questions:
Krystal Lee Enterprises
Email: sales@KLEPub.com
Contact: Phone: 770-240-0089

To Reach the Author:
Email: me@authorklee.com or me@drkrystallee.com

Web: Authorkleecom
Social: IG, FB, Twitter, TikTok, Youtube
@AuthorKLee

Printed in the United States of America.

Disclaimer
The information in this book was correct at the time of publication, but the Author does not assume any liability for loss or damage caused by errors or omissions. These are my memories, from my perspective, and I have tried to represent events as faithfully as

possible.

Acknowledgments

I extend my gratitude to everyone who has supported me during my development. It's with that same heart that I present this second book in the Embrace Your Crown Series to you.

Thank you to my children, family, and Royals with the Embrace Your Crown First Sunday's Meetup Group!

To my incredible Father God (Yah) and my Savior Yashua the Christ, thank you for entrusting me with this powerful series to impact lives.

Shalom (Peace and blessings) to every reader.

Table of Contents

Dedication	7
Introduction	17
You Don't Need Magic	23
Make Room for Miracles	43
Know the Promise	65
Dare to Dream	85
Kick Negativity	107
Tack Courage	131
Transform Go Beyond Change	153
About the Author	157
Resources	159

DEDICATION

So, Why Did I Write this Book Series, anyway?

Life has a way of changing things, doesn't it? We can be five, fifteen, twenty-five, and fifty-five plus, and at each phase of life, something different becomes necessary. As we live, we learn that mastering life could take a lifetime. Those who say they have figured it out can go through a challenge overnight, and life doesn't seem as simple anymore.

We can get in the swing of raising children, and then they grow up and move on to live their lives. Sometimes, we get settled into our marriages, and divorce or death breaks up the union. Or you get the news that you are pregnant, and all of your single days are behind you. Other times, it could be plans we have for the future that go up in smoke because of a layoff or termination.

Life is unpredictable. We realize we cannot control all aspects of our lives, and I wanted to give people something to help them adjust to the waves. This three-part series was created because one book wasn't enough to deal with everything we feel and experience that makes us hesitant to *Embrace Our Crown*!

In Book One of this trilogy, it's the heart. Many of us do not know all the areas of our lives that were impacted by life's changes. We can think of burying what has hurt us and trying to forget, but the pain is under the rug. The more we shove things under the rug, the bigger the lump gets. It is easy to walk over it for a few years, days, or weeks at a time.

What we don't see is how matters of the heart impact how we spend our time: the way we define our purpose, how we develop patience, and what patterns we are accustomed to. What our wants and desires are were greatly impacted by the atmosphere we grew up in; it matters. Crazy enough, the lifestyle you have forged might be completely based on a straw version of you and not your divine makeup.

We have all been hurt and we learn to adapt to change as best as we can in the moment. That is fine, but temporary circumstances should not blindly guide your life. You want to find the root cause for why you believe and act the way you do. Some of our habits might have been forged from pain; and if so, the way we see ourselves might not be accurate.

Opening the 7 Gates to Find and Overcome Heartbreak is crucial because it helps you get to the root of an issue. I learned that I was a great problem solver because I wanted to prevent my stepfather from yelling at me. I became resourceful out of necessity and fear. This helped me in my business, but it came back to bite me in my relationships.

Not all the habits we pick up are inherently good or bad. Moments that broke my heart, I learned that the incident had both positive and negative effects on my life. I needed to learn what made me good at being Krystal and also what my Achilles heel was. There is a pattern if you have a string of failed relationships, lost opportunities, jobs that didn't promote you, or situations that constantly repeat in your life.

The only real question is, do you want to change the pattern? If you want to see the ins and outs I share for how I opened these 7 gates and learned to look at my issues head-on, read the first book in the series after this one, *Embrace Your Crown: Open 7 Gates to Find and Overcome Heartbreak.*

Dedication - Embrace Your Crown

Book Two, E*mbrace Your Crown: Open 5 Gates to Overcome Unbelief*, is a goody too! If you are starting the series in this book, you are in good hands. When you can envision your purpose and know your calling, the first thing coming your way is doubt. The enemy is clever for having you take your eye off the ball and confuse your mission by saddle-bagging you with emotions that suck out your zeal to succeed.

If success felt easier than failing, more people would succeed. When our hearts are heavy, our ambition can be weakened. When we cannot see past the trees, it can be hard to stay motivated to fight through the storm up ahead. As Celena tells me, life is a challenge either way, so you must believe in something worth fighting for, or you will merely exist.

Within the pages of this book, I am going to show you that you first don't need magic to win in life. If you are not a lucky person, you are in luck. You don't need luck to walk out your life with the help of God. He doesn't work by wishing on a star, for how many good notes you wrote to Santa, or how good you have been lately or all your life. Yah is a mystery because He picks murders, messy people, people with faults, regrets, shame, and dirt on their name, and He cleans them up!

He wants us to come as we are so He can clean

us up. He wants your pain, problems, frustrations, doubts, thoughts, and fears—to put your burdens on Him because His shoulders can carry your load. When we realize how big God is, that's when we can make room for a miracle!

Miracles are gifts from God, moments when He steps into our lives and performs a task that only He can do. He permits His power to enter the realm of our reality to shift things in our favor. We have all heard favor isn't fair--but how do we get this favor? Is it by crying, yelling, fighting, trying to bargain with God, or something else? How do we obtain the favor of Yah?

I'm glad you asked. Go to Gate number two, and I will share more. Also, in this book, we have to Know the Promises of God. Knowing what God said about you is important. How are you a child of God when you don't know what He said to a child of God? Being royalty and not knowing the boundary lines of your kingdom sounds crazy, right? How are you a joint heir with Christ, and you don't know what you have access to because of Him?

Do you like that song, "Everybody Ought to Know?" I used to sing it all the time as a child growing up in church. I absolutely loved it, although it was a very short and simple tune. Some of the lyrics I liked or can remember:

Dedication - Embrace Your Crown

Everybody ought to know, (repeat)
Everybody ought to know, (repeat)
Who Jesus is, (repeat)
He's the Lilly of the Valley,
He's the Bright and Morning Star,
He's the Fairest of Ten Thousand,
Everybody ought to know!

That is the whole song, and I sing that song like the never-ending song on Lamp Chop! I absolutely loved it and could sing it on repeat. Scan the QR if you want the melody to sing when things are crazy in life, or your children need something fun to learn and do! I had a solo in church, so I remembered my part, but the other person didn't remember theirs, so I sang my verse twice. That might be why I don't know the whole song, lol.

SCAN THE QR TO

LISTEN: EVERYBODY OUGHT TO KNOW

The other three gates are Dare to Dream, Kick Negativity, and Take Courage. I know implementing these five gates is not easy, but I assure you the journey is worth it. The labor is one of love and reading—not too shabby, right? Plus, you can join me on social media to check out my posts about *EYC* and other helpful nuggets along the way.

Yes, there is an Introduction that gives a bit more meat before we dive in. But now is a good time for us to connect so I can share some bonus video content with my Royals, you! Yes, you are Royalty; you are a Queen or a King, and I want to break it down for you! Scan to add me to your phone and send me a text, or follow me on social media at @authorklee on all platforms (FB, X, IG, Tiktok, Pinterest, LinkedIn, Youtube)

SCAN THE QR TO CONNECT ON SOCIAL
ADD ME TO YOUR PHONE!

Okay, I'm almost there. In Book Three, *Embrace Your Crown: Open 3 Gates to Sharpen Your Focus*, I wrap up this series. By no means is the journey over; that's why I have the First Sunday meet-up group: life will keep going on. The books are a guide to help you point to the gate, but mastering the skill and implementing what you learn is a journey.

The good part is that I am committed to you on this journey to share my experiences and helpful connections along the way. Knowing you are not alone helps you stay committed. Have you ever gone to a gym with a partner who would push you when you kept pushing the snooze to get up and get there?

Dedication - Embrace Your Crown

I am that person for you!

When you jump into the third book, we are sharpening our focus. The first thing we are looking at is why are you so deep in the water anyway. Why do you care so much if you succeed or fail? Why do you pray and do the things you do? And if you don't, what should you be doing to get back on track?

We can all get weak and weary in well-doing. It is not limited to the ones without the intention to do good but also the "do-gooders" and "in-betweeners." Sometimes, we are tired of doing right when things seem to keep going wrong anyhow. We can think to give up and save ourselves the trouble, but are we in fact, saving ourselves or losing ourselves?

Lastly, I want to show you that your purpose is not the same at every phase of life. If you are here, there is a reason, and we owe it to Yah, ourselves, and those following behind us to find out. Don't leave this earth full of life nor full of regrets. Leave empty, and put it all on the table. Try what you want to accomplish, and don't be so focused on your desired outcome but the journey. Perfection is not the key to happiness.

In the words of Melvina, "There is a whole lot mo," but we gotta get going on this book so that I can park it here. This trinity of books is meant to interlock to help pave a way forward for those searching for their way out of inadequacy, fear, a drought season, frustration, depression, doubt about the future, and those praying for miracles to find hope!

Your life can change, and I believe that by reading what you already have, you feel lighter. That is good, and I want you to continue to explore that as we move on. Allow your hope and joy to come back. Search your heart with the section wrap-up after each chapter. Consider coming to my First Sunday Event at 4pm Online or connecting with me at a live event. You can scan the QR, go to EmbraceYourCrown.com for series content and events or InviteEYC.com to attend *Embrace Your Crown* First Sundays meetup group.

Cheers to the many who are in pursuit of happiness, joy, and growth. May this series richly impact your life. I believe it will and I encourage you to grab the three-part series to ensure you don't miss anything. Did I mention that this series makes a great gift year-round?

I jest, but if you want to get the series and

share it with others, use the QR for a special price offer on my website, AuthorKLee.com (it's on Page 2 of the store.)

SCAN THE QR TO
ORDER THE BUNDLE

Introduction

"For the vision is yet for an appointed time, but at the end it shall speak and not lie; though it tarry, wait for it because it will surely come; wait for it." Habakkuk 2:3

In life, we can easily feel out of place and think that because some things tarry, they will not happen. I know as the years tick upward, we can't help but look at the clock. Like standing in line for long periods, we can get bored with waiting. The wait sometimes is more brutal on our mental than our ability to do something.

There are many things that are in our control, but it seems like twice as many that are not. The key to life, I have learned, is to do what I can and pray about what I cannot. Before we do anything, I sug-

Introduction - Embrace Your Crown

gest praying because you want to know that your direction is sure. Believing you have the right thing(s) going helps to put life into perspective.

What happens in life during our wait varies from person to person. Some of us grow frustrated, others grow weary of well-doing, and yet others lose faith. We start doubting our abilities and whether we heard correctly. We think maybe I got this wrong, which is why what I thought wasn't happening.

We know the fault isn't with God or His ability, so we start to point the finger at ourselves. We start to question if we have what it takes, if now is the season, or if we messed up somewhere and the delay is punishment. Have you ever felt like something was off in the grand design but didn't know where to point the finger?

I, too, have felt this way many times. We can be confused and start to doubt when the things we have hoped for don't happen when we expected them to. These occurrences can lead to a broken heart. The Bible says a heart deferred grows sick (Proverbs 13:12). Are you sick and tired of this drought that is playing cat and mouse with your emotions?

Is this game with your heart, tossing it from hand to hand, or has it shattered in a million pieces because it fell? Our heartbreak isn't limited to romantic relationships that fail. We go through heartbreak because life can be difficult sometimes. People can say things that cut deeper than a knife. An eye glare or a simple "humph" at the wrong time can send a tsunami of feelings to your heart and thoughts to your mind.

Too often, we may feel foolish or silly bringing up things that break our hearts. We are taught to forget about our pains and bury our issues, believing we are becoming stronger in doing so. But unresolved issues only delay our future.

Have you noticed that an old issue pops up in your future every now and again? If we are honest, we can point to daddy issues, mommy issues, broken relationships, failed expectations, loss, and even death of close people we love and care about. It can be downright hard to live life and not be knocked off our cloud, can't it?

The truth is, we are not robots. Although we may want to ignore the things that have happened to us in the past, many of us relive our past every day. This is why your pain is so strong. You learned to adapt to survive, but now you are stuck in survival mode and don't know how to switch gears.

If you are still dealing with unresolved heartache, it could feel like you are chasing an invisible enemy because you can't see it, so you can't say who it is. For some of us, the enemy is ourselves and how

Introduction - Embrace Your Crown

we have changed to overcome our pain. If you want to achieve your goals in life and see a clear road forward, you have to be honest with where you are in life.

You have to consider whether you are still on the path or if you are carrying dead weight that keeps your future far off. When we have unresolved issues, we try to live our best lives despite the limitations of how we learned to adapt because of heartbreak. In book one of the *Embrace Your Crown series, Open 7 Gates to Find and Overcome Heartbreak*, I teach about the seven gates that are impacted by heartbreak: Time, Purpose, Patience, Patterns, Wants and Desires, Atmosphere, and Lifestyle.

I share my life story and give examples of how you can see the same or similar problems I had to overcome because of heartbreak. We don't get it all together even after learning what has hurt us over the years. Your journey starts there in this three-part series because often when we lack vision for our future, our glass is too blurred by our past. So you, typically, start in that book, and if you don't have it, no worries, you can start here–but I encourage you to get that book and discover the nuggets I have for you. If you missed the Dedication starting on page 7, check it out. I share a bit more of all three books and their connection.

Now, because you are here, you are ready to

overcome the limitations of your unbelief. Unbelief is a sneaky problem we all face, and it tries to come back and point to your inadequacy, challenges, and limitations in accomplishing your goals. This book will deal with the reason you struggle to believe in yourself, your goals, or your dreams.

If you are slow to accomplish the plans that God (Yah) has for you, I am glad you are here right now. In this book, we will discuss Miracles, Dare to Dream, Knowing the Promise, Kicking Negativity, and Taking Courage, all to Transform and Go Beyond Change!

Though your vision, dreams, prayers, or prophetic Words for your life tarry, it will come. The plans for your life will be established, and what the Father promises, He will deliver! Let's have a conversation that will help you accomplish the plans our Father has for your life!

Introduction - Embrace Your Crown

YOU DON'T NEED MAGIC

You Need Power!

"My flesh and my heart may fail, but God is the strength of my heart and my portion forever." Psalm 73:26

If you are like me, I bet you enjoy tv, scrolling on social media, or watching a good movie that can transport your thoughts away from reality. This is the point of television and videos, right? To create a world that people want to spend ten minutes, an hour, or more watching. Some business modules are based on you binge-watching content and creating something so irresistible, you will be back weekly to catch the next show.

In years gone by, this was the norm for everything. We had to wait for the things we wanted. We couldn't turn on the tv and find all of the shows already loaded; we had to wait for it. The same with food. When I was growing up, there were only a few chain restaurants around that offered fast food. We didn't get it often because my mom had to cook; money was funny as the saying goes.

When you don't get something often, when you finally get it, it is like getting a prize. Fast food, I have come to find, is not better than home-cooked meals. It is convenient, but I cannot say it is as memorable as a good home-cooked meal! Some things I have learned that take time are better because they took time.

Although meat cooked at a high temperature might be well done, it can easily burn on the outside if the flame is up too high. Essentially, the outside will fire up before the inside has enough time to cook. The juicy steak or delicate inside with a crispy, enjoyable outside can be completely missed when we move too fast.

Are there things in your life right now that you are turning up the fire to cook faster? The truth is, you need to respect the process and "let it cook!" (My daughter Kayda introduced me to this phrase and I had to use it. Don't mind my pun.) Not everything was meant to be cooked in the microwave, though. In fact, there is much science to prove that microwaving anything puts poison into your food.

You would think that if there were even a slight study of what can happen to our bodies with these contraptions, we would easily put them outside of our homes and ban them altogether. But are there things we cherish more than our health? Do we enjoy having a quick solution over having to tarry for a solution?

Remember that some of us had to go to the library and study for days to get the information we needed to finish a paper. Today, students can go to Google and start searching. There are online sites like J Store that make even finding articles faster than years prior. You don't need to thumb through books; you can do a search with a title and pop up tons of results.

Has this quick access blurred our ability to appreciate good standards and values meant for life? Have we gotten so focused on the end results that we no longer care about process and quality? We know using and doing things can cost us our health, but the convenience and easy fix are addictive, aren't they? Is it a wonder why our generation would rather have magic than power?

Magic is attractive because it requires no effort to manifest a result. How many of us would love for a fairy godmother to come in and swoosh her wand, and our house would be clean? Maybe we want to mend our relationships. We don't want to talk it out; we just want the issue to disappear, to forget it ever happened.

We want the results without having to do the work or wait the time it takes for it to cook! How many of us know that if we cook a cake too fast, it will fall flat? If you shake the oven door, or if your patience gets the best of you and you keep opening the door, you will continue to deflate your cake because you were too anxious to wait on it.

How many of us think that bombarding heaven with complaints is moving the needle in the right direction of change? Magic is often an illusion. It is not real magic that mesmerizes us when we see tricks performed. It is our desire to see something that mystifies us. We really want a miracle, but we might not have the discipline to make room for it, so we settle for magic.

Magic is a lie. It is an illusion, a distraction, a slight of the hand. One thing is happening, and while you are focusing on that, another thing is happening in plain sight. While we are expecting God to move here, we are not looking at what is happening over there. We are so focused on what is in front of us that we cannot see two paces beside us.

This tunnel, or limited perception, doesn't help us in one sense, but it can expose where we are in life. If you feel like you need magic, something to happen spontaneously to change what you don't have the discipline to change, what you need is power!

Feeling powerless and deflated can make us want to give up. It can make us think we have wasted our time and that what we are working on has no value. It will make us seek external factors, even against our best judgment, to make a change in our lives. Desperation can make us do strange things, can't it?

It is when we realize we have a form of godliness and no power that we need God the most (2 Timothy 3:5-7). But the flesh, our minds, and even some of the advice we hear can attempt to point us to external things that can magically change our situation. We can tell ourselves we need money. But a fool and money will soon depart (Proverbs 21:20).

A person who doesn't have any knowledge of what to do with money. When they get more of it, they will blow it. Plenty of millionaires who got spontaneous money end up broke every year. Do you know most lottery winners end up broke after winning millions in five years? Most high-paid athletes and artists, after they stop being relevant, don't have enough money to sustain a lifestyle they grew to love.

The Bible says, "Wealth brings many new friends, but a poor man is deserted by his friend" (Proverbs 19:4). How many of us, when we had more, yes, we were not lonely, but the people who surrounded us were not genuine. When we have good health, the people who sucked up our time are no longer around when we are in poor health. The people who said they loved you, you can't find when you are in need–but when you have, they are the first ones ringing your phone.

What about influence? People will tell you if you get an influencer, you can get more. Isn't it funny that when we apply worldly tactics to certain parts of our lives, they don't work? Getting an influencer to help you sell something on social media is a marketing tip anyone would give you. How many of you know that not everyone with influence is worth listening to? Some smoking advertisements are still paying the price for influence.

Many of us got caught up in something because we were influenced to go in that direction. We must, however, look at the results of influence. Everything is permissible, but not all of it is profitable (1 Corinthians 6:12).

Although we can do anything our heart desires, and can listen to who we like, not every voice should we give a say in our decisions. Not every promise made to us is worth paying attention to. Some promises that you made even need to be broken. Some influences on your life need to change. Some money you have or can make is not worth the cost of having it.

If right now you feel you are short on cash, influence, knowledge, or power to accomplish the plans the Father has for you, I can raise my hand and say not so! There have been slaves who came up and won against incredible odds to make things happen—people who were born into countries stricken in war that made it out to safety. There are too many stories I can list that prove we can overcome with little to nothing.

So they didn't need money, people, or anything outside of their belief to start walking in the power to achieve the plans God had for their lives. I said it before, and it should be repeated: "You have everything within you to transform your life! You were born on purpose, with a purpose, for a purpose."

You might feel you need something special to

get to the next step, but I assure you, what you need to achieve your goals is power to overcome your unbelief! You need real power–not things, magic, that make you feel you have power. Money can leave, people can, circumstances can change, and you will be back to square one without real power.

When we don't do the work to acquire lawful power, we might settle for thinking we need magic. If you think you need an outside and foreign power to take your life to the next level, let me tell you that you don't. What you need is the Presence of God that gives you power!

What has been fighting you is not natural. You might say, "Yes, it is Krystal. It is the bank who told me no." "My husband said he wants out." "My children want nothing to do with me." "My bank account is speaking to me, and it is saying insufficient funds."

And I hear you. I have been there before, too, and so I can attest that people and circumstances speak to us–but do you know who is speaking through them? We are not fighting flesh and blood but principalities and systems of darkness (Ephesians 6:12). You are encountering an attack, and being a child of God means you are subject to the enemy seeing you as a threat.

What you are in hopes of achieving is a threat to the enemy's camp. What you want to do with your marriage is a problem. How you want to raise your children–and how you see yourself is putting fear into the enemy's camp so he tries to get you distracted with things–magic.

We have to remember the world is real. If you feel fire, it's hot. If you feel the wind, you can be moved. If you hear a voice, you don't need a face to see the lips moving to know you are being called. You can hear the voice. The Bible says that Yah's sheep can hear His voice (John 10:27-28). Can you hear Him speaking to you in the midst of your storm?

The spirit realm is real. We are so certain that the natural exists because we rely on our main senses, but the one we all use the most and don't pay as much attention to is our sixth sense. We can all agree that we have deja vu; we can feel like a place is familiar or a moment in time, but we don't have a natural reference point.

We don't try to explain it because we can't. We sometimes think that we are having day visions or dreaming while awake, but what if you were seeing in the spirit? What if what you so easily dismiss is what is trying to connect with you? What if you are too busy to see the spirit realm and settle for magic? Would you be okay with the substitute?

It is a poor substitute for the Presence of God. We can be guilty of underestimating the power of God because we attribute His glory too often to ourselves, circumstances, or situations. How can a man rob God and is it possible to rob someone who is not here to lay claim on what is His? We rob God every time we withhold from Him what is His (Malachi 3:8). It could be financial, time, your heart, love, affection, or attention.

When we take these things from Him and

give them elsewhere, we are robbing God. What happens when you steal from someone? Do you look for justice? Report the crime? Expect retribution and to be made whole? How long should He wait to be in your presence?

Humanity has us thinking we were made, and God is here to make our dreams come true. That God was made for us and not us for God. We are not the center of our own existence. Many of us have not seriously asked God why we are here. How should I honor You today? What He wants when we are young can be different, and it will change over time as we mature. When we stop talking and listening to God, He will permit blocks in our lives to help us to sit down and see what He wants.

He could single us out like Job and encourage the devil to try our faith. We want "to try Jesus," but we don't want Him to try us. We say we believe, but do you believe enough to tarry, to go through, and still trust Him? Real power is built through endurance. It is a learned experience that works power and commitment.

Where you spend your time is where your power comes from. What is your source? What feeds your thoughts, ambitions, hopes, dreams, or fears? We watch tv, and we see superheroes, and they all have a source for where they get their strength. You can get your power from clean energy or dark matter.

Clean energy, the light, is fueled by the Word. Enter into His gates with thanksgiving and His courts with praise (Psalm 100:4). Is your power coming from magic? Is it powered by your pain, disappointment, frustration, fear, or anxiety? These emotions, spirits, are strong enough to push you ahead, but you won't work for the light. The gifts they bring will come with heaviness, darkness, and emptiness.

    For many of us who have everything, if we lack the Presence of God, what we have starts to lose its value. Having gained the whole world but losing your soul can make you resent what you have (Matthew 16:26). It allows you to see the cost, and you might find that you don't like it. You want out, and wanting out doesn't necessarily mean giving up what you have, but you want clean hands, a clean heart, and a renewed spirit (Psalm 51:10-12).

    This is salvation. This is saving grace. He can make our yolk about our neck easy and our burden light (Matthew 11:28-30). The yolk about your neck is to direct your path. How can two walk together unless they agree (Amos 3:3)? You cannot be directed by someone who you are not willing to follow. If you are not willing to walk with God, how can you be a follower of God? If He says wait, and you don't want to, you are taking His yolk off when you stop waiting.

    He says His burden is light. Many of us are heavy-laden, but He can give us rest (Matthew 11:28). There is nothing too hard for God Almighty to fix. I know we have some difficult situations with family, friends, finances, marriages, business, and the stresses of life. I know magic is more tempting than working to be in the Presence of God. The temptation to get something for nothing–how many of you know something for nothing usually costs you a higher price than the value of what you get?

We learned nothing in life is free, but everything costs you something. If someone tells you, you can get something for free, how many of us know the rule? The first time is free, but the next time will what? Costs you! The devil is a liar, and all of his tricks include lies, destruction, manipulation, and confusion. He uses these tricks and antics to steal the glory from Yah by getting you to come away from His Presence.

When we go after magic, we reject the power of God and settle for the power of dark magic. We are going to feed our selfish ambition and work for our own cause, forfeiting the plans Yah has for us. But what does the enemy do when he is done using us? He will cast us aside. He loves to see our children hate us. He wants your marriages to fail. He wants you to feel down, lost, hopeless, powerless, and lean on pain for power.

Let me be clear: you don't need magic! But You Need Power! Your strength is not outside–it is within you! Greater is He that is within you than he that is in the world (1 John 4:4). It is God Almighty who you want to give you power to gain wealth (Deuteronomy 8:17-18). We were all given powers from the Most High. Fallen angels used their powers to corrupt man, but you can use your power to give Him glory. You can choose to endure to the end and remain in His Presence, obtaining power from heaven.

You can yield your power, which is your soul–mind, will, and emotions. You get to choose what you believe and how you will live your life. When you feel like you are running low on power, you need to tap back into His power because no good thing will He keep from you (Psalm 84:11)! Don't give any more power to the enemy, the power of darkness, but give glory to God today. Allow Him to pull you out of darkness and into His marvelous light (1 Peter 2:9)!

To be in the Presence of God, you have to allow Him to direct your path. For you to receive power, you have to spend time. You have to make a conscious decision to put God first. I know you might say, how can I? In the same way, we make time for the things we want to do that are away from God; we can use that same mind to spend time with God.

Life will fill our lives with things to do. I am sure everything on your to-do list has a purpose, and you can defend why it needs to be done. By the same token, we know the things we have to make room for and the things we left undone for months or years on end. Why do we avoid the things we don't want to do?

Is it because they aren't easy? We don't like the process? Or performing the task doesn't please us. I know when I first started reading the Bible, I would fall asleep. It took no time, too. I would get to a few verses down, and I would be gone until the next morning. I am embarrassed to admit that, but that is where my journey began.

I would read and forget everything I just read. The devil was having a field day with my attention span and memory. I honestly thought maybe the Bible was too difficult for me to understand. I started buying other translations to see if that would help. I still fell asleep, but I did better when I got the Chronological Bible.

I enjoyed reading the Bible in the order of publication believed by scholars and historians. It helped me formulate a running story that I couldn't place with the King James Bible alone. When I started to see the Bible in a big picture view, it was easier for me to find enjoyment in reading it.

I didn't care too much for the names in the beginning; honestly, I struggled with them a lot. I liked the principles I was able to dig out with the help of Billy Hall, my first mentor. To grow in reading the Bible, you just have to keep doing it no matter how little you read each day. I wrote a 21 Day Devotional and Journal, *Bless The Works of My Hands*, to help those who struggle with spending 10 minutes a day with God.

SCAN THE QR TO

ORDER BLESS THE WORKS
OF MY HANDS

For those of us who didn't grow up in church or were over-churched, finding a relationship that you establish with God is critical for your development. We cannot lean on someone else's understanding and connection with God to solve our problems. Yes, people can pray for you, but after a while, God and them are expecting you to pray for yourself.

The power is not theirs, the pastors, your mother's, or your prayer partner's; it is God's Power. If you need a miracle, change, or progress, you need a relationship that is your own. You need your own source and access to God Almighty. You need to know that you, too, can come to the throne of grace and ask for what you need.

The Father of Creation doesn't get bored or tired of hearing about you. He says to cast your burdens on Him because He cares about you (1 Peter 5:7). How you are being treated, how you feel, and what you hope for, He wants to know. There is a difference between telling the Father about your problems and giving glory to them through complaining. If we cannot be honest with God, how can we be honest with anyone else?

He sees everything that happens on earth, thought in our minds, or actions in our hearts. He is the one who can solve our issues and speak to people's hearts. For those who need a banker, a doctor, or help of any kind, He will give you favor to not need a person if they won't be used by Him to bless you. That thing called grace that we all need, He gives it to all of us so we all will be without excuse.

Patience is a virtue, and it is learned and not given. We learn how to wait for the things we hope for. If you are asking Yah for something and are not willing to be patient for it, working each day, you may not really want it. Having a baby takes nine months of work. Then, when the baby is born, it takes your entire life to be a mother (or a father). We don't get to retire at an age, but we serve differently. We grow.

As you grow, God is bigger and able to go through any phase of life with you (Isaiah 40:31). When we are weak and unable to see how a thing is going to get resolved, it is in our weakness that He is made strong (2 Corinthians 12:9). You need to be reminded that you can do all things through Christ who strengthens you (Philippians 4:13). You can forgive, earn wealth, achieve milestones, re-establish relationships, believe in yourself, and the list goes on and on.

As you focus on what you can work on as we conclude this chapter, "Focus on the importance of recognizing that God can provide strength, even in times of difficulty or trouble" (Isiah 41:10).

Thinking Points!

    A.   Are there areas in your life where you are harnessing your power from pain?
    B.   What problems have you identified that you want God to help you solve?
    C.   Do you feel that you have taken glory that belongs to God in your life?
    D.   What changes do you feel you need to make to help you walk in Power?

Now, I want you to do the Self Check-In to *Embrace Your Crown*!

  I. Let's Check You In!
    A.   Situation
    1.   Are you prepared to lean into the Presence of God and allow Him to shape your patience?
    B.   Change
    1.   To welcome the change you want in your life, are you prepared to start a growth journey with God to help you through your troubles?
    C.   Endurance
    1.   As you start to lean on God to direct your path or recommit your time and hope to His lead, what verses can you use to remain hopeful and stand in faith for change?
    D.   Persevere

1. If the process feels like it is taking some time, I want you to create a journal entry to remember where things were in your life before God. Consider what He has already done to keep you hopeful for what is still to be done in your life.
E. Acknowledgments
1. We don't always have all the right answers or do the right things. Sometimes, we fall asleep waiting for God and can feel He is taking too long. We can be honest about our feelings but also allow the Word to guide our hearts. Our hearts and minds can deceive us, and as humans, we can be flaky, but God is constant and steadfast. Remember to place His Word above your feelings so you remain in power.
F. Re-Purpose
1. If you have felt you were missing things and that is why you are struggling in life, take the time to see that the Father may have allowed the rain, the drought, or a breakdown to happen to bring your attention to an area. It might not get fixed

overnight; it could take years, but don't give up on what He can and wants to do in your life. Though it tarry, wait for it, and the Father will give you peace.

G. Help?

1. If an aspect of this chapter was difficult and you want to talk about where you are, please do. Be encouraged; you are not alone. We have free and paid resources to help you work through this series. Skilled coaches, therapists, and speakers are here to help.

Sometimes, we get stuck in a process or want to discover more about what makes us or has made us who we are. Do not feel like you can't linger on a thinking point, question, or chapter. If you need help throughout this book at any point, I want you to contact me and my team. We are a network of coaches, counselors, and prayer warriors ready to help you Embrace Your Crown, connect the dots, and go from where you are to where you are born to go.

Dr. Krystal Lee

H. *Embrace Your Crown* Affirmations: Let's make some declarations!
1. I was born on purpose, with a purpose, for a purpose!
2. God Almighty is my source, and I will not use pain to achieve gain.
3. I choose to live in the light and draw my Power from the Presence of God.
4. I will be honest about my feelings but also subject them to the Power of God.
5. In my weakness, I am made strong through Christ who strengthens me!
6. I will not seek out magic or try to get something for nothing.
7. I will make time for God and put Him first in my life.
8. I am willing to follow God's lead and be patient to endure.
9. I am ready to *Embrace My Crown*! Embracing who I am and who I was born to become!
10. I am ready to TRANSFORM and Go BEYOND Change!

You Don't Need Magic - Embrace Your Crown

MAKE ROOM FOR MIRACLES

It Requires Obedience

"The signs of a true apostle were performed among you with utmost patience, with signs and wonders and mighty works." 2 Corinthians 12:12

If you haven't heard this before, likely it is because your cape is in the cleaners. You are a superhero! You have the power to do many things because you were made in the likeness of God (Genesis 1:27). You were born with gifts, talents, and things that the Father wants you to use for His glory (James 1:17, Romans 12:4-8).

He wants us to tap in so we know how to bless Him with our gifts. The fallen angels also have gifts, makeup, time, music, and on and on. These angels didn't lose their power when they fell from heaven when they decided to change their source. They decided to feed on darkness and rob God rather than serve Him in the light. All things are beneath God's feet.

As joint heirs, they are beneath you, too! But they will use your complaints, pain, and powers to give glory to darkness. If we are not lifting up God, the light, we are lifting up darkness. The Father's heart is to bring you into the light, into his magnificent presence. It is easier to be in the Light than to be in darkness.

Darkness is heavy. Depression is heavy, dark, and void of joy. Why should anyone live like this when God offers the gift of mercy, grace, love, and long-suffering to heal and restore us? He wants us to think on *good* things—things that build up and not tear down. He wants you to see the good in everything because His purpose is to make everything work for your good (Romans 8:28). The enemy cannot change Yah's plans, but he tries to circumvent them.

I remember one time hearing my mom tell me a story of my aunt. I don't do scary houses because I just don't do scary! Hahah, I have really intense dreams and I know I travel and see things it is hard to unsee if I am entertaining things I shouldn't. I don't even like the zombie shows from this modern age or anything that involves dead people moving around for an apocalyptic theme.

Have you noticed that these movies are heavy? They feel dark, and the feeling of doom can quickly absorb your energy. You have to think or get something in the light just to change your mood. I don't like feeling like this, plus I know that scaring the wrong people can end up in violence.

Have you seen the reels of people trying to scare folks, and they end up getting punched out? All things are fun and games when you know it is a joke, but can you imagine any of these pranks being played on you? I would absolutely not like it–though it can be funny to watch. My aunt almost went to the hospital, messing around with a spooky house many years ago. She ran up a slide and started swinging on anything coming in her direction.

She was still on so much adrenaline that after they turned on the lights and the cast washed the paint off their faces; she still was breathing hard. They sent the guy who scared her the most and suffered the most punches home with pay. My mom and I laugh about that to this day because darkness is scary, and it does two things: dull our senses or arouse fear.

When we go to movie theaters, they also attempt to immerse us in the movie by turning down the lights. Turning down the lights triggers your mind to be less alert. One thing I hate is a dark church. I can watch sermons where people are on the stage preaching in a dark audience, but I would not want to attend weekly in person. I love the light, and club-like atmospheres with strobing lights are not my thing.

I feel like some aspects of modern ministry are a distraction. Of course, not everything that happens in the dark is bad. Babies are formed in the womb, and it is dark. The Father created the light and the dark and considered it good (Genesis 1:4-16). If the Father wants to work a miracle, He can choose to do that in the dark, too. Many would say, it is what you do in the dark, when you think no one is looking, that demonstrates your true character.

Not everything we do in the dark is good. If a person wants to hide, they hide more easily in the dark. The devil will work in the dark, the dark spaces of our hearts, minds, and emotions where we may think to hide, to block or delay the Father's timing. He will manipulate us into speaking words that make us a pessimist rather than an optimist. He will try to get us to curse ourselves and operate out of a low, dark spirit. He will make us feel like victims, not good enoughs, or losers. But we WIN! If only we knew what the plans are that the Father has for us.

The enemy's job is to keep us in the dark so we can see magic as what we need. The devil is good at bringing the things we want to us, so we stop believing in miracles. He wants us to have to sacrifice to get magic instead of living out obedience and being benefactors of something far greater.

He is the counterfeit of what the Father has designed for us. The enemy wants you to think you can only get things through magic and working hard for it. How many of us know about favor? Wave your hands if you know what a miracle is. Can you use a miracle in your life? It begins with the Power of God working through His Presence.

We all pray for miracles! When things don't

look good, and you feel you need power from on high, we lean toward a miracle. Miracles are cute movie ideas. They can be grand and make us feel warm and fuzzy, or they can be simple and have a special place in our hearts. The miracle many of us need is deeper than a Christmas gift under the tree or a prayer answered for snow on Christmas Day.

Many of us need to be witnesses of the Hand of God because if it is not for Him, we stand no chance to change the situations in our marriages, with our children, hearts, minds, lives, businesses, and careers. Those of us with a ministry or hosting an event constantly pray for a miracle. A miracle could mean people showing up or buying our product after we went all in or all out to make it happen.

Sometimes, our expectations are higher than God's, and other times, they are lower. We may start something without really understanding the commitment it demands. We can easily believe there is no more left in us, so we try to tap the power that can make great things happen in the twinkle of an eye.

But what if I told you that miracles are not random? Do you think it is about luck and you being a favorite of God for why you can be in a position for a miracle? Miracles, signs, and wonders are supposed to follow us. That is what the Word says, question, are they following you?

I don't care about the size of the miracle, but do you see that the Hand of God is on your life? Do you see Him showing up for you? Have you noticed the key ingredient for making room for a miracle in your life and that of others?

He says we can have a form of godliness and no power. We've learned that the Presence of God is the key to opening these 5 Gates to Expand our Unbelief. Without the Presence of God, it will be impossible to hold the weight of these gates open alone. It may work for a while, but how many of us know that working a miracle is not natural?

I told you, magic is not natural but is a use of dark powers to draw strength. Miracles are the product of working power through your obedience. Have you noticed that when you make a covenant, or a vow, with God, He takes that very seriously? The Word says it is better not to vow a thing than to vow and not do it (Ecclesiastes 5:5).

What does a vow work in us or force us to do? It forces us to consider our faithfulness or the lack thereof. We all know of scriptures that point to the Father's faithfulness toward us. A popular song that we all can sing, one of my favorite versions of late, is by Melvin Crispell III, "Great is Thy Faithfulness." This song is rooted in Lamentations 3:23, which reads, "Great is His faithfulness; His mercies begin afresh each morning.

SCAN THE QR TO

LISTEN: MELVIN CRISPELL III
GREAT IS THY
FAITHFULNESS

I say to myself, The LORD is my inheritance; therefore, I will hope in Him!"

There have been times I needed a miracle in my life, like you. I remember I needed to move, and I didn't have not only the money but also the credit. When you have a late payment or a reported debt, getting another apartment is practically impossible. If you have read my book *Look For the Drip and Expect the Outpour,* you would know I have been a beneficiary of many miracles.

SCAN THE QR TO

ORDER: LOOK FOR THE DRIP AND EXPECT THE OUTPOUR

I can tell you that they all have followed my obedience and faithfulness. When we are obedient, we find ourselves in God's will. When Moses was faithful to do what the Father commanded him to do and confronted Pharaoh to let His people go, He gave Moses the power to do so (Exodus 5:1, Exodus 9:1). Notice that he didn't take away the issues Moses had. He didn't give him perfect speech but allowed him to keep the stutter (Exodus 4:10-14).

We can want Yah to remove the things we think make us blemished or unsuitable for the road ahead. We can find inadequacy in our abilities and see issues with our disabilities, but these ought not be the reason we stop believing and pursuing a miracle. Building a relationship with God is required by all creation, including those who appear "normal" and those who have challenges.

I love a good friend and client of mine's testimony, Melvina. She was born with a nerve loss that cost her 50% of her hearing. Growing up, it was hard for her to hear anything and fit in. She was deaf as a child. Wearing hearing aids and going to school wasn't easy. She got made fun of, and her physical attributes didn't help.

She complained at home about being called names, and her parents gave her some advice. Her mother said pay them no mind and work on giving them grace. She assured her that she was beautiful not to believe the insults the other children said. Her father told her to be great. No one can deny your results.

SCAN THE QR TO

LISTEN: MELVINA W
"GIVE ME SOMETHING TO
WORK WITH"

It is hard to forgive people who are not sorry. At the time, the children didn't apologize and she would have been waiting until her adult years to get one. It is difficult to want to befriend people who make fun of your pain, so the road can also be lonely. She learned to build her relationship with God and allowed Him to establish the confidence she needed to make it in life--through her parents first.

This woman's miracle was embedded not in her natural healing but in seeing that she, too, could be anything she wanted to be. She had to *Embrace the Crown* that was hers and not focus on what was for everybody else. Our miracles might not look like everybody else's expectations of healing to assimilate, but for you to remain you, and stand out. Sometimes, they need to learn how to love others and see all the people God loves through seeing your flaws. Our weaknesses prove it is not about us, but about God's power to use anyone no matter their flaws.

He said that before He formed us in our mother's belly, He knew us and ordained us for a purpose (Jeremiah 1:5). Before you were here, God Almighty had already spoken a Word concerning your life. He had already fashioned a purpose just for you and made a plan for how He would help you make it happen.

The Father values His Word so much that He made it the structure for all creation. He created everything that is, through a Word! His Word. We don't live off bread alone, but from every Word from the Most High (Matthew 4:4). I can attest that every miracle I have ever enjoyed came at the behest of committing my life and doing the work–not to earn it, but to show my heart towards God.

I know we are all mindful of people who want to use us. We have this radar that goes off to tell us, "Check that one out. They might not be genuine." So we test them. We are cautious around them. We want to see the fruit, the actions the person takes, to determine if they are, in fact, someone we want around us.

Now, the Father knows all things. He knew you before, and He knows your beginning and ending. Nothing about you will come to Him as a surprise, but what will surprise many of us, is to find out just how much we care about Him. We all think we are in good standing with God or our beliefs until we are shown ourselves.

Some of us find out through this faithful test that we are not faithful. In the little things we do each day, if we are honest, we are not obedient to make room for a miracle. You see, the Father says it is the good things we do that can build us up or tear us down (Proverbs 12:2); the little foxes spoil the vine (Song of Solomon 2:15). When we are in our peak and life is going well, how you respond is the fox. It can come to tear up what you planted. It can be sown to cast doubt on what you have. It can be a distraction that draws you away from what to focus on.

Miracles: I love them because they help us remember what being a child is like. When we are a child, we are quick to believe for a major miracle. We put it all out there when we pray, don't we? We ask for things and put in specific details. What happens as we get older, though? We begin to restrict our prayers and start to ask for stuff like, "Lord, please make a way out for me. Father, send me a husband." General prayers can expect a general response.

There is nothing wrong with being simple. I feel like I am a simple person. I am not big into designer things. I am practical. I am okay with shopping at Goodwill, the same as at the mall. I believe both locations can work, depending on what you are trying to do. Some people are content if you give them Goodwill, while others have different expectations.

Is one wrong over the other? No. People have different requirements, and we cannot be mad about our desires. The Bible says to delight in the Lord, and we can ask Him for the desires of our hearts (Psalm 37:4). It's okay to have a big dream and desire a miracle. But also be willing to commit to what the Father wants to work that miracle in your life.

If He asked you to fast, pray, or study for a month, would you do it? If He wants you to spend time with Him so He can have a relationship with you before the marriage, would you? Do you know the blessings or miracles He sends our way can send us away from Him? Maybe your miracle is held up because of your lack of faithfulness in an area. I raise my hand to say, at one point, that was me.

I wanted to make some relationships in my life workout so badly. I thought because I had invested in them, that God wanted me too also. Some people in our lives are there for ministry. These people can be attractive, and that attraction can make us lose focus on the real picture. The Father is faithful in giving us an escape before a problem worsens in our lives. I moved past all the red flags, believing that my disobedience, my sacrifice, would somehow make Him happy.

Have you ever went too far to help save somebody? I tried marrying someone and dating another for years, only to be the one bruised and more lost than I began. It took soul searching to get me out of the mess, and that was the miracle! He pulled me out, cleaned me up, and helped me to believe for better. Some day, I plan on marrying in the future, but for now, I am celebrating the miracle of surviving the past. I am glad I don't look like my past or carry bitterness about it.

What about you? Are there areas in your life where you can be honest and say, "That thing right there is not making room for a miracle?" What if you are praying a mist? Could that be why your prayers hit and miss? Or could it be that you don't have a relationship with God, or it has gone cold, and you are more like a distant relative who comes only for the holidays to talk to God?

Remember when Peter was on the boat with Jesus (Yashua)? As long as Paul kept his eyes on Jesus, he could walk on water (Matthew 14:22-33). As Peter kept walking on the water, the bold faith he started with manifested the miracle. It created steps of water under his feet! But as he traveled, the thoughts, the doubt, and reality kicked in, and he began to sink. He began to sink into the ocean!

Do you know how dark it is underwater? There are parts where you cannot see an inch in front of your nose. You feel the coldness, you can sense the dark, but you are not at peace like how you can have looking up at the sky and seeing the stars. This feeling is cold, lonely, and screams save me. When we take our eyes off Yashua, we start to lose our direction because He is the way.

If we are out in this world and things stop working for us, if we stand in need of a miracle, have we taken our eyes off of Jesus, and that is why we cannot see the miracle? Miracles, signs, and wonders are here every day. The Bible says God's mercies are new every day (Lamentations 3:22-23). How can we miss them? Maybe because we stopped looking for them.

When the enemy sabotages our efforts, we cannot move our eyes off of Yah. We cannot forget what we are working for: to be obedient to the Word, to hear the voice of God and follow Him, to believe what He said about us getting married, having a business, healthy relationships, and living a good life. We have to know what He says about us and our situations.

When I was a new believer, I knew I confused mercy and grace with miracles. I thought the things that happened by supernatural means were all miracles. I remember being dead wrong in one way or another, but the Father still extended His hand to deliver me. I consider that a miracle. What I didn't know was that it wasn't a miracle, but mercy and grace.

When we are living a life contrary to what the Father has for us, He can choose to have mercy on us. He says I have mercy on whom I choose to have mercy (Romans 9:15-16). When we get what we do not deserve while we are still working through following His voice–or if we haven't committed to follow Him but He guides us anyhow, that is mercy.

His heart toward us, when we are not thinking about Him because we are hurt, in pain, feel rejected, low, angry, or sad, is grace. His desire to love us when we are unlovable and unfaithful is grace. By His grace, we receive something we did not deserve. Now you see how I got the two confused? I thought I needed a miracle, but what I really needed was grace and mercy to be obedient so I could make room for a miracle in my life.

My circumstances didn't dictate the Hand of God. He can be the reason we are sitting at home and not working. He can choose to send somebody to jail so they are not busy doing whatever but can hear from Him. Sometimes, He sends your children out of the house because when they were there, they brought you no peace. He says He will give you peace, and sending people out of your life can be the miracle you didn't ask for but you need.

The Father is not Santa Claus but the Creator God, who knows what you need and how He made you. How many miracles we have experienced unaware because they were things we didn't ask for? I love the song that Ruben Studdard sings, "I Need an Angel."

I love this song because we can carry burdens that are too heavy for us, and we want help! We need something; we can see the finish line and the trees in the distance, but it is too far for us to reach. There are things in the way that block our vision. We say, Lord, I need to get higher, I need an Angel, I need a miracle. Something, send it on down right now, Father!

He really gets into singing when he says, "Send an angel down right now, Send an angel on down right now..." If you haven't heard the song, play it today. It will definitely lift your spirit. But this song spoke to my heart every time I heard it. Even writing this book now, I can point to a few reasons I need the Hand of God in my life.

SCAN THE QR TO

PLAY: RUBEN STUDDARD
"I NEED AN ANGEL"

Life on the surface is good. Bills are paid, business is going well, and I am on the road to fifty books–currently on book 32! Yet, I believe God can change things for other people, which requires a miracle. Have you ever wanted something so badly for someone else? The doctors haven't fixed it. You see your friends or neighbors getting worse seemingly each day. You wonder if your prayers are helping or harmer things.

It can make us weary in well-doing if we don't see our prayers answered sooner rather than later. I can tell you that I have had prayers answered quickly and others that tarry. With either outcome, my joy is the same. If you are believing for things that have not yet come, don't give up.

Don't give up on your business, your children, your future–don't give up on God! I know it can be hard to believe when things point to reasons for why you should throw in the towel. We must keep moving because this builds our endurance and belief.

You know something I like about the ant? The ant knows how to keep working while it can because there is a day coming when it will not be able to. These insects remind me that miracles can be a result of stored-up obedience. The Father says He will not be indebted to no one; He will repay those who have given up something to follow Him in this life and the one to come (Mark 10:29-30).

We cannot be so focused on the natural things on earth that we think they are the most important of all. How many find out when they die that this life was a testing ground for eternity? We are to be like the ant, working and being diligent because one day we will not be able to–for whatever reason. We don't want poverty to creep up on us because we are idle. This idleness can be spiritual poverty—lack in relationships, time, food, money, wealth, or the Presence of God.

"The poor will be with us always" (Matthew 26:11) has come to mean so much more to me as I have lived longer. I used to think it meant money and being economically poor precisely. Now, and over the last handful of years, it has come to mean so much more. Poverty can come and it is not your fault. You can lose a job, lose a person, lose hope, lose the will to carry on. Being poor in spirit can come as a result of no fault of your own.

Being at a loss like this doesn't make you lazy, stupid, or rejected by God. In fact, it makes Him draw closer to you. Jesus knows what it is like to lose someone. He cried when Lazarus died (John 11:35). He walked the earth and felt everything we have on the cross and through His experiences.

It takes faith and power to walk this life, and it is not always easy. I know I have heard it said that the reason people become believers is because they are lazy or afraid to work. They don't work hard enough or want something bad enough, so they lean on religion. Not true. Sometimes, nothing can be harder than having faith, believing in something you have not yet seen.

It is easy to lean on your money and say that you don't need God because you can work for what you want. But what happens when you can't? What happens when the world shuts down, like in the years of Covid? We all needed a miracle to make it through it, didn't we?

Faith is not easy. We have to work even without seeing; it takes power to live by faith. We have to work in the spirit and believe in God's existence and power. We have to understand that as we are obedient, we are working power. If you want to make room for miracles, you have to have faith in the Word of God. You must believe in His Power!

Thinking Points!

    A.   How are you spending your time in the dark? Are you focused on good things?

    B.   Would you consider yourself a faithful servant of God? Do you have a schedule that helps you remain accountable?

    C.   Do you feel right now in life you need miracles, mercy, or grace? It's okay to want all three!

    D.   How are you feeling about your overall health? Consider the situation in your relationships and if there is anything you may need to pray about.

Now, I want you to do the Self Check-In to *Embrace Your Crown*!

  I. Let's Check You In!
    A.   Situation
      1.   In your life currently, what areas are you desiring God to touch?
    B.   Change
      1.   What changes do you feel you can make to help you get into right alignment with God to make room for miracles?
    C.   Endurance
      1.   Becoming faithful to start and complete a vow with God is the first step to work confidence in your relationship. What commitment can you make to God

now that you will work toward?
D.   Persevere
1.   Forming a new habit can be difficult. It can take 21 days to form a habit. If you fail or start to lose focus, don't stop. When we learn to keep going when we want to quit, we are making this process about God and not our own emotions. Persevere!
E.   Acknowledgments
1.   Whenever we do something new, it is challenging. Don't be quick to beat yourself up if you need more time or are not perfect. I wasn't perfect, and it took time to get to where I am in God. Be patient with yourself, know God loves you, and keep going! I am still a work in progress, too!
F.   Re-Purpose
1.   As you formulate these new habits in your life, it can be easy to get down on yourself about how you used to be. If today is a new day, yesterday is in your past! Choose to make everything work for your good like the Good Lord wants for you.
G.   Help?
1.   If an aspect of this chapter was

difficult and you want to talk about where you are, please do. Be encouraged; you are not alone. We have free and paid resources to help you work through this series. Skilled coaches, therapists, and speakers are here to help.

Sometimes, we get stuck in a process or want to discover more about what makes us or has made us who we are. Do not feel like you can't linger on a thinking point, question, or chapter. If you need help throughout this book at any point, I want you to contact me and my team. We are a network of coaches, counselors, and prayer warriors ready to help you Embrace Your Crown, connect the dots, and go from where you are to where you are born to go.

H. *Embrace Your Crown* Affirmations: Let's make some declarations!
1.   I am learning to be faithful because my God is faithful!
2.   I will have a lifestyle that Makes Room for Miracles.

3. I have the power to change my life and the lives of those around me through my obedience.
4. I remain grateful for the miracles, signs, and wonders that follow me all of my days.
5. Today I say thank you for the mercy and grace on my life!
6. I will not give up on my purpose even if temptation and dark times are ahead.
7. I will keep my eyes on Yashua (Jesus) as I move forward in life.
8. I will not jeopardize my future to save someone else but will help through obedience in Christ.
9. I am ready to *Embrace My Crown*! Embracing who I am and who I was born to become!
10. I am ready to TRANSFORM and Go BEYOND Change!

Make Room for Miracles - Embrace Your Crown

KNOW THE PROMISES

You Are Not Alone

"I will instruct you and teach you in the way you should go; I will counsel you with my loving eye on you."
Psalm 32:8

Have you ever had a chance to sit in a lounge chair at the beach? If you have, you are familiar with the rolling of the sea off in the distance. The gritty sand under your feet finds its way in between your toes. The beach can be relaxing, calming for our nerves.

On the ideal day, the sun is out and waving to you, kissing your forehead and giving you enough heat to keep warm as you enter the water. If you play on a surfboard or stay in the shallow parts, the cool liquid that gently washes over your feet is welcomed as the sun beats down. Sometimes, that low rippling wave can be the refreshing you desire to cover your body, even your soul.

You feel calm, and although it would be easy to feel restless at the beach, the feeling is not lazy. It is…peace. You don't mind hearing people off in the distance. You are fine with the random stray birds that fly or call in the background. You may even return to your towel-covered lawn chair after playing in the water and lie down. You can lay there if you have an umbrella or the sun is in the right place.

You feel free when you lay there and take in the sight and hear the ambient noise. You are at rest. Wouldn't it be nice if you had this same feeling away from the beach? If you could find this inner peace that truly transcends the noise buzzing around your heart and mind. If you could shift away from the anxiety you feel daily–even for a moment, how could that impact your life?

The Bible tells us to be anxious for nothing but to put our cares on God (Yah) (Philippians 4:6-7). Do you feel you can, or do you, cast your burdens on Yah? Imagine if you were having a meal at a restaurant with God, would you offer to pay the bill so you owed Him nothing? Would it make you feel better about your decisions because you didn't use Him, you wanted His company, but you don't trust His direction?

Are we guilty of dating God and not wanting to marry Him? Calling Him the one who got away and not the one we are in love with and desire to never leave? Are we capable of showing that kind of love to anyone? To the point that if we thought He would leave, we would come begging on our knees for Him to stay.

Some of us are on our knees doing everything but praying and casting our burdens on Yah. Some of us lay our burdens down but pick them up before we leave. We say things, think things, and pray things that cancel what we believe for. Our anxiety about waiting causes us internal pain and strains a relationship that is able to give us perfect peace and rest.

When was the last time you genuinely enjoyed being in the moment with Yah? When you weren't thinking about the next move, watching tv, listening to music, or doing something else to fill the silence? Do you know the Father sometimes wants you in silence so you can be in the moment? The same way we find enjoyment in the things He provides by nature could be how we stop our worries and anxiety to hear His still voice in our hearts.

When we are tuned in to God, we can block out the birds, the sand, people chattering around us, and the things that used to easily distract us. Our focus is heightened because we are in expectation. What are you expecting? Do you have expectations of God, or do you expect because of God?

We are to keep our hearts, minds, eyes, and souls focused on good things (Philippians 4:8-9). Things that build up and not tear down. Things that edify, build up, encourage, and inspire (Romans 14:19, 1 Corinthians 14:12). Are you encouraged today? David said if no one else is doing it, I will encourage myself (1 Samuel 30:6)!

With what power could David fight a Giant? With what power did he overcome his enemies and adversaries? With what power did David take back everything that belonged to him? With what power did King David receive the blessing that goes from generation to generation? Was it his perfection? No. His faithfulness? No. But his heart. David is a man after God's own heart (1 Samuel 13:14).

Who's heart are you out to capture? If it is the Father's, we have an example of His faithfulness toward man. David was far from perfect. He stole a wife. He murdered. He plotted. He leaned on his own understanding. He failed his children. And the list could go on and on; our list of sins could too, but Yah! He said He chose David, the least, and determined to make him great (1 Samuel 16).

It is not through your efforts or your wrongs that we are prized by God. It is not by our education or how well we speak; Moses is an example. It is not about how much money we have; King Saul had no inheritance before becoming king. So the key to accessing the promises of Yah is not based on your strengths, but your weaknesses (2 Corinthians 12:9).

The areas you allow Yah access, He enables you to take on His likeness and power to overcome all things (Luke 10:19). John 16:33 says, "I have said these things to you, that in Me you may have peace. In the world, you will have tribulation. But take heart; I have overcome the world."

But do you have peace? Do you know you can take heart because the Word has already overcome the world? Do you know His Word is so faithful, it is a promise. What He speaks will come to past–every Word (Isiah 55:11). Are you believing the promise? Can you see it in your life?

Or do you feel like, "I know you said in my weakness God You are made strong, but I don't see that. I don't see that there even is a God with how much hell I have been going through. My children reject me; my job is on the fritz. My business could be better. I work hard and bring little in; I feel like I am cursed and not blessed. What do you mean believe for a miracle from God? I am struggling to see God, let alone believe in God."

You don't know that He will have your enemies bless you (Deuteronomy 28:7-9). He will fight your battles and win them always. Those who thought to curse you won't be able to, no matter the efforts they make. Who can curse those whom God has not cursed (Numbers 23:8)?

When we see pain, drought, and devastation surrounding us or the uncertainty of government, jobs, finances, economics, and social norms, it can rattle our foundation. But you are more valuable than the birds that fly in the air or the grass that grows that someday will be consumed (Matthew 6:26-27). The Father knows the hairs on your head, so how can He miss the problems you face (Luke 12:7)?

Could it be that we are not rooted in God? We are shaken out of place by the earthquake of problems in our lives, and the foundation has shifted. What broke up our foundation? Was your faith built on answered prayers? Was it built on sinking sand, a relationship that has faded away? What was your anchor? The promises of God?

Or is it your understanding of His answers? What He allows that we agree or disagree with? We wonder if His ways are really better than ours or those in the world. We start to look at others and say, "They ain't Christian. They're not believers. Look how well they are doing. What happened with me? Why am I not blessed if I have God on my side?"

There are statistics to help support your nerves and fears, as well as facts. How many of you know that God can overcome facts? Facts come about through actions. Actions create facts because they are the outcome of a forced or natural response.

The enemy loves to divide and conquer. He loves to put people against each other for anything. In war, the opposing force always looks for a weakness to reduce numbers and better their odds of conquering. If a government, country, or family is too strong, you start by taking out the weakest link. You try to get them out of position, hoping they will bring the whole team down from within.

The Bible says a foolish woman tears down her own house! How many of us have seen family members do more damage than an outsider? A husband more than a thief. A wife more than a hooker? The enemy loves to use us against each other because pain creates the best criminals, witches, and people who will tap into dark power (magic) to gain in life.

In isolation, you can be conquered. His goal

is to win your soul–he wants your will. He wants you not to have the will to do right. He wants you to not believe any other way is possible but this way. He wants to cut you off. He wants to corner you in your mind in hopes that, breaking you down piece by piece, you will conform to his plan and abort your purpose to give God glory to please yourself, which is selfish ambition.

When we walk off and leave our place in God to follow after painful trauma or allow the enemy to pin us mentally to traumatic events, he can reduce our ability to think out the right solution. Out of fear and pain, we will react, but not all of our responses are good. He wants to use your emotions against you to pin you in a mental hell that keeps you from embracing who you were born to become.

He can't take what God has for you, but he will do his best to convince you that it doesn't exist. That if you do not work and sacrifice, you can't make it or will not have enough. He convinced Adam and Eve they needed more, and he wants to trick you all the same. To have you believe sacrifice and works of your own hands are more important than obeying the Word of God. He has no new tricks; he's the same old devil with the old tricks who is trying to pull on the same emotions of our ancestors. He thinks he knows you because he knows of you.

The enemy came to Eve because he thought she was easier prey. The devil took them out one at a time, but God is bigger and can fight groups. The mountain Moses went to, he was invited by God. Those who saw him come down, saw the glory on him from being in the Presence of God. They thought to have that for themselves. They wanted what Moses had until they started to feel the cost.

To learn God is not just about reading a book; it is living the Word, practicing the Word we read in the book! He didn't invite the others, but in their own self-righteousness, they counted themselves worthy to stand on holy ground. Can you imagine what Yah told Moses? He probably said something like this: "I didn't invite them, but let them see what it is like." As they got to the foot of the mountain, they stopped.

They looked at Moses as they stood at the foot of the mountain. Seeing his imperfection, they thought they were better. They weren't murderers. They didn't stutter. They were walking in the desert, the same as him. If they had the stick in their hands, it would work for them like Moses they thought!

How many people think by looking at you, or you looking at them, that if you had their position, you would get the same outcome? But how many stop at the foot of the mountain and grumble about you even though they ask you to pray for them? They see your faults and don't marvel that God can save them all; they get envious instead and seek another way to get glory without God. They erected a golden calf to idolize.

How many have fallen short of Yah's intentions for them to settle for what their hands could build–what they could catch with a tight skirt or who they could trick with their lips? People who don't know you can only associate what they know of you. He said He came to set the captives free; the Pharisees missed the message (Luke 4:18). Death is already paid for, and sin is already paid in full (Colossians 1:14). This is what has already been done, already said, already a promise fulfilled–but do we know?

Do you know that once you have been charged and tried for a crime, you can't be charged again for the same crime? To be charged twice for the same crime is "double jeopardy." The enemy wants to accuse us of our past and make us believe we still have to face the challenges that are promised, as punishment for sins that have already been forgiven. Don't give into double jeopardy; know that the promises of God are faithful and the Word is mighty to save (Isaiah 63:1, Zephaniah 3:17)!

In a fallen world, the victim is in chains. The felon who pays their debts has a rap sheet that follows them. They are labeled and pushed into a corner to keep living life as felons long after their debts have been paid. How is this not double jeopardy? But in a fallen world, dark, gross darkness, this is permissible and even defended as righteous.

This is dark. When Barabbas was set free, there was no police report following him. The enemy will use any system to bring out gross darkness, the evidence of living in a fallen world. Feeling injustice. But God promised to make way for your escape. The devil didn't know what the plans were for Yashua; he didn't know who He was, or he would have tried to stop Him from fulfilling the promise. What if you, like the Messiah and angels (Hebrews 13:2), are hiding in plain sight?!

What if everything in your life is on purpose? What if the Father wants you to experience life so that you can bring His light to problems? What if we are to use His promises to inspire, encourage, and change situations around us? The enemy is confused, so he looks to you to determine what God is doing. He is still lost!

He can't chart God's moves, so he tries to get us in doubt and out of position so we won't receive whatever there is for us. The heart of God and His Word should comfort us. 2 Corinthians 9:8-10 says, "And God is able to bless you abundantly, so that in all things at all times, having all that you need, you'll abound in every good work. As it is written: 'They have freely scattered their gifts to the poor; their righteousness endures forever. 'Here are things they only find out by watching you."

You see? I told you, you had power. This is a promise, a Word concerning your pain, troubles, and distractions that has you in disbelief for the plans God has for you. Although we don't know all the details, we must be confident of His power and promises. This is your power, and Yah is the source of your strength.

How can we have a form of godliness and lack power? If you lack His presence, you lack His power. His power is mighty to save, and if You don't have the Word, there is no salvation. If you have power without results, you have gifts, talents, and knowledge without the touch of Yah's blessing—as His children, we abide in His house, His rules. We can speak about how the enemy treats his children, but we are not them.

You serve the King of kings, and even for what looks like a loss is a win for you. You haven't *Embraced Your Crown*, if you don't believe in the God that saves and helps you abide, Jesus the Living Word who gives you power. What has the enemy told you in your mind, made you feel in your emotions, or crippled your will through depression, doubt, and discouragement?

What is blocking your belief? Belief is spiritual and is not natural but manifest in the natural. So as a man thinks so is he (Proverbs 23:7). What are you thinking about? You need to know you are not alone in your thoughts.

The Word is for you, and the Presence of God is with you. He promised to never leave nor forsake you (Hebrews 13:5). He is so good even if your bed was in hell, He is there with you (Psalm 139:8)! There is no pain, no hurt, no sin, no trauma, or no disappointment He cannot deliver you from.

Peter began to sink when he took his eyes off the Word (Matthew 14:22-33). The ocean is dark as you fall into the belly. If you are in a dark place, you have to fight with your emotions, will, and mind to abide in the light.

When we become new creatures, old things pass away. The devil's job is to bring you back into the dark space. To keep you ignorant of his devices. The enemy's hope is that you won't remember the promises of the Father (2 Corinthians 2:11). He wants to use your pain trauma to isolate you and indoctrinate you so that you will reject the promise of salvation. He wants you to doubt the power or the potency so you will try and coexist with the limitations of living carnally.

We are ignorant of the enemy's devices when we don't read, study, and pray. We don't know his tactics and what we accept, thinking it is life could be the enemy stealing, killing, and destroying things in our lives. He wants to isolate you, so you won't pray for your children. So you won't be around to advise them on how you beat the devil. So you can be in your feelings and say they can figure it out alone. He wants you to be abandoned and abandon others.

But the Bible calls us to help each other bear each others burdens. How are we going to do that if we don't talk? If we don't see each other? If we don't pray? If we stop going to God or give Him thanks for fixing it. Some things have gone south over years, decades, or half of a century. Why do we think God has to be a microwave problem solver, or He doesn't work?

What if we have fault in how we communicate with others that brought on the pain others spew at us? Is it not His prerogative to correct both guilty parties, not because of what you have done to each other, but how you both have offended Him? He is a good Father, one who is a just judge, who knows everyone's heart and can separate bone from morrow

(Hebrews 4:12). He knows your heart and true intentions (Jeremiah 20:12).

The enemy knows if you are in a group standing with God. He cannot corral you into the gates of hell. He cannot break you if you form a three-chord strain with God the Father and the one you are in a relationship with. If you form your relationships in the hands of God, you will find things will work themselves out.

It is a process, and you will need people to lean on. If you are alone and relying on your own understanding, it is no coincidence that you will struggle to believe God's promises. If you cannot accept the Word of God, you will not have a promise to stand on. The Word of God gives you Power!

You cannot fight the devil with emotions. Anger without righteousness is dangerous for humans (Proverbs 27:4). The Bible tells us to be angry but sin not (Ephesians 4:6). For many of us, we cannot be angry and hold back sin, and the Bible acknowledges that too (James 1:19-20). So Yah tells us to remain in joy. The Father promises to speak to us so that we may know what we need and may take on His joy and confidence (John 15:11). He will keep us in perfect peace and give us rest (Isiah 26:3).

The Bible says in Ephesians 6 to put on the whole armor of God. Why do you need armor unless you are under attack? As believers, we are under attack, fighting powers that are coming for our souls. The Bible says we must work out our own soul salvation (Philippians 2:12). What you believe in your mind, what you define as your will, and controlling your emotions are your choices and lessons to learn. We have to live the Word we hear, the Word we believe, the Word that saves us. We need weapons that are not carnal to fight a spiritual battle (2 Corinthians 10:4).

Humans in a superhero fight are so weak. Have you seen how the monsters, we will call them demons, toss them about? We look the same when we are trying to be carnal and operate our businesses, lead our families, and live a holy life without the ***power*** of God. We can think all is well because we don't see the danger. But that sixth sense keeps you uneasy. Don't be quick to ignore the radar. Don't ignore it, but seek direction and guidance when you feel it.

If what you are doing is not working, trying another way might be the best move. The Father has given you the power to shape your life through His Word. The Word is living and a being, it is who Yahshua (Jesus) is. He says I have given you power to cast a mountain into the sea by faith (Mark 11:23-24). I have given you the power to use my hands (Deuteronomy 8:18). The Word has given you the power to achieve greater works because He sits at the right hand of the Father (John 14:12).

The Word is fighting for you, defending you, and interceding for you. We cannot ignore His saving grace. The decisions we make and how we respond to His promise to save us from all sin either saves our souls or cost us our souls. The Messiah came here to set the captives free (Luke 4:18). He came to be a ***sav-***

ior and a ransom for many (Mark 10:45). We need Him to open our lives, expose our inadequacy, and ask Him to give us beauty for our ashes (Isaiah 61:3).

As a ***redeemer***, He essentially pays the penalty for your shortcomings and restores you whole, meaning you owe nothing. You owe nothing to your past, but you owe all you can give to your future, to what changes you can make moving forward. You cannot be held in the past; that kills what your future could become.

You need the **_Savior_** if you need things to happen in your life. You need the One who came to help humanity. Many in the Bible rejected Christ when He came because they thought they didn't need Him. They wanted things–magic, businesses, government, houses, countries, land, and things that were tangible. But only the Messiah came to restore your mind, will, and emotions. He wanted to fix you so that you can be in right standing to pursue God and achieve the purpose of your life.

If you put first the Kingdom of righteousness, everything will be added to you (Matthew 6:33). By giving your life, you save your life; by trying to keep your life, you lose your life (Matthew 16:25). In our lives, we have to be careful that we don't celebrate the benefits of our relationship with Christ and miss the gift or promise. The Father promised us the Messiah because we could not atone for our shortcomings. He gave us a living example because we didn't know how to live the Word no matter how hard we tried.

He knew we needed grace, and we all still do

today. He brought grace here; He knew we needed healing, and He brought that here. He knew we needed love, and He made love in the flesh so that we may touch it, hear it speak, and feel Him wrap His arms around us. We need love, we need power, we need the ***Savior***. But what are you looking for? How are you trying to close the gap in your heart?

We are looking for many things. We are looking for a banker, a business, a husband, lashes, purses, bags, and houses. We are looking for tangible things, and the lust for these things can lead to compromise for our souls. I often ask what it is that men could want so badly that they would sell their soul and give up their will, mind, and emotions to something else.

When people choose a life of sin, they are not giving up things: empty vessels with no heart, mind, or emotions. They are given up their legacy, battering their futures and canceling their hope and love. Love does not abide where hell is high. The Father turns His face from sin (Isaiah 59:2). He hates it. He hates to see us succumb to something beneath Him. We are His prize, His people, created for Him.

You are part of the promise for humanity. Your life matters. *Embrace Your Crown*, **Queen**. *Embrace Your Crown*, **King**. Your purpose and legacy are needed in the Kingdom of God.

Thinking Points!

A. What promise have you read that has given you life?
B. Is there someone you need to talk to to clear the air in a dispute?
C. Do you have the Savior working in your life to do what you cannot?
D. Do you know what bothers you, bothers your Father?

Now, I want you to do the Self Check-In to *Embrace Your Crown*!

I. Let's Check You In!
  A. Situation
  1. Have you been trying to do all the work on your own and things are not responding the way you need?
  B. Change
  1. What can and what will you do to impact this aspect of your life?
  C. Endurance
  1. Making changes in your life is part of our growth journey, so what is something you can think on to motivate you to keep the process going?
  D. Persevere
  1. There will be challenges up

ahead; but don't allow the storm to keep you from believing the promises of God concerning you. You are not alone and His plans for you are good no matter what you see or how you feel. No matter what comes, Persevere!

E. Acknowledgments

1. If you feel like the promises for your life aren't happening or taking too long and those around you are falling as they wait, be encouraged. Our purpose is intertwined in the body of Christ. We are all needed to accomplish the great work of God! Keep believing, Love.

F. Re-Purpose

1. If the promise is still being worked, take comfort knowing God will be indebted to no one. He will repay in this life and the one to come. You will always win and He will redeem all time lost. Shalom.

G. Help?

1. If an aspect of this chapter was difficult and you want to talk about where you are, please do. Be encouraged; you are not alone. We have free and paid

resources to help you work through this series. Skilled coaches, therapists, and speakers are here to help.

Sometimes, we get stuck in a process or want to discover more about what makes us or has made us who we are. Do not feel like you can't linger on a thinking point, question, or chapter. If you need help throughout this book at any point, I want you to contact me and my team. We are a network of coaches, counselors, and prayer warriors ready to help you Embrace Your Crown, connect the dots, and go from where you are to where you are born to go.

H. *Embrace Your Crown* Affirmations: Let's make some declarations!
1. I am blessed no matter the mess I see or pain I feel!
2. There is a purpose locked in on the inside of me and I am working to see its manifestation.
3. Although the enemy thinks to discourage me with challenges, I will choose to trust in Yah.

4. Greater is He who has plans and promises for me than what I am experiencing now.
5. Today I accept I need a Savior and I will allow Him to direct my path!
6. I will choose to believe your Word everyday!
7. I thank you Father for choosing me when I did not choose You.
8. I will commit to spend quality time with you every day building my reverence and trust in You.
9. I am ready to *Embrace My Crown*! Embracing who I am and who I was born to become!
10. I am ready to TRANSFORM and Go BEYOND Change!

DARE TO DREAM

Is to Believe

"Truly, I say to you, whoever says to this mountain, 'Be taken up and thrown into the sea,' and does not doubt in his heart, but believes that what he says will come to pass, it will be done for him." Mark 11:23

It is no mystery why many of us don't dream–forget dreaming big–but at all as adults. We are bombarded with thoughts and opinions, usually from family members, early on to be realistic. "Pull your head out of the clouds." "Think about all that stuff later; you need to focus on life right now."

The very words meant to encourage and set us free can turn to the ball and change that keeps us removed from faith. That holds our dreams in the clouds and keeps us from believing for them. When we pray, we pray a mist because we don't believe (James 4:3). Faith the size of a mustard seed in due season will produce a tree, but if that small faith is not even there, what will become of it?

    We have all heard various versions of these phrases that pop our balloons that were holding our dreams. Instead of them going up into the air and probably reaching heaven, we allow them to come tumbling down to the ground with an uneventful impact. We say we are being realistic, but honestly, something within us dies. Faith dies within our hearts and our hearts are broken; many of us keep on moving in silence attempting to disguise our silent suffering as power.

    When your dreams hit the ground you don't think about things that stretch your imagination anymore. You focus on what you can see and what seems real, as in happening now, to define what you can believe for the future. You can base your entire future on a limited perspective of your now, and how many of us grow to hate that shortcoming?

    You know when a guy you were thinking of talking to, only you didn't because they didn't have it all together when you knew him. Maybe he was young, building, starting over, or just seemed too messy for you. You couldn't see his potential, like how many cannot see the value or maintain an interest in a fixer-upper.

    We often want people and life situations to already come ready and prepared for us. No matter our shortcomings, we are expecting the best. We may secretly sabotage our outlook thinking on what we can see or believing we need the things we can see because having faith for the greater is asking for too much!

Have you ever felt that faith is harder to muster up than a good work ethic? I mean, believing in things hoped for–even when you are not seeing—is a conundrum. How are we to live in the world and disregard what we see in front of us? How are we supposed to keep believing for what has not yet manifested–and for many of us, we don't have a twinkle of hope that it is on its way?

Hope deferred makes a hard grow sick (Proverbs 13:12), is it a wonder why so many want magic–or even works to help them justify their life's choices? Doesn't it make us all sleep better at night when we have locked all the doors? When we are dating someone who checks all of our boxes? If it does feel so good, how is it that too many of us grow to dislike the very reasons we like someone? How do we miss the huge red flags before we commit to long-term relationships and commitments?

How do our attitude and confidence shift? Why are we no longer content with the boxes they checked but can become resentful? We think, "Is this all life has to offer? Or is there more to life that I have missed?" We wonder if we made a mistake on the list or in our review and missed a flaw or line item.

The truth, no matter what a person looks like today and how many boxes they check, time and circumstance happen to us all (Ecclesiastes 9:11). We can have a job today that is gone tomorrow. Looks today that can be washed away in the sink. We can have a glimmer of something we want, only we were being safe because we were hurt before by something we desired. So we think to want nothing and accept what is safe.

How many of you know settling for less will always make you feel like you are settling for less? We grow to hate what is safe because, deep down, we all love faith. We love serendipitous moments. The thrill of not knowing something good is around the corner when you are expecting it. When it is your birthday and you know some people in your life are up to something, you don't know what, but there is a unction in your belly that something is up.

You go through the day expecting, not clearly of what. You check your phone looking for anything out of place. If nothing raises a yellow or red flag, you keep searching for the clues. How is it we can do this for things, people, events or circumstances, but we fail to do this with God? We fail to see the value in faith, the good in waiting with expectation.

We think that we are foolish to wait around for God when we have two hands, a mind, people, family, and resources. So we try to go it alone, only, our efforts don't always hit the mark. We think life could have more and we used to believe that, but something has choked the life out of our belief so we are left to wonder. We lean more on hope, but not in God, we resort to wishing upon a star!

We say prayers wishing that this or that comes true. "I wish things were different," we can be quoted for saying. However, have we ever considered our faith was too weak to have hope in God to make a change? It can be hard to keep believing when you are not seeing. Wishing instead of having hope might feel like you are doing Yah a favor by letting your expectations down a bit so you are not disappointed if He doesn't deliver.

Can you imagine the emotional instability of a child who thinks to ask their parent for something only they have already decided that it will not happen? In their hearts, they have already accepted the answers and are only going through the motions. They have no heart to believe for the good, they don't dare to dream because their reality has already erased their hope; but be encouraged.

Why should you keep your eyes and heart set on dreaming and expanding your belief? Because this is the hope that will give you power for when you are weak, weary in well doing. This reduction in hope is a knock on your faith. Do you know faith the size of a mustard seed can cast a mountain into the sea (Mark 11:23)? Do you have that kind of faith?

Can you believe something so grand, bigger than a mountain, and want something so wild, for that large mountain to be moved into the sea? Do you believe Yah wants to do big things for you, your family, your business, and your situation? He wants to work a miracle but can you believe–have hope and faith for it?

I know, you are facing something big, something personal, something pressing. If we could snap our fingers and the situation would resolve, many of us would go for magic–but the devil has a price, too. The currency of heaven is faith, the currency of working with the enemy is getting wants and desires without patience, faith, and temperance (self-restraint).

When we lack the patience to wait on Yah, we will take matters into our own hands and make bargains with ideas we don't know the extent of the connection. If you feel like you have bit off more than you can chew in an area of your life, simply meaning things have gotten out of control in your life, you need to dream bigger and extend your hands. You need a miracle, a life change, or a new wind to come and saturate your heart and mind.

Since when should we keep our hands closed into a fist thinking we can help feed anyone? A closed fist is not in posture to bring the good news anywhere. You need to receive before you can pour out. You need something to pour in, to renew you, possibly to correct you, so you can share that love with others. We have to open the gates that have led to our heartbreak and be encouraged to overcome them! We can and must overcome!

It is hard to dream big if you are stuck thinking too small. When we accept things how they are and leave the game with a loss, not realizing it is one game and not the season, we can miss open gates to change our lives. If we are okay or passive about the things being taken from us, we can grow comfortable with any temperature. As the water heats up, we can naturally adjust to the water we sit in. We can be dying inside like a slow-cooking frog or lobster, unaware of our demise.

K. Lee

Have you ever sat in water and it was good and toasty, but as you kept sitting, the water-cooled off? The dirt hovered and clung to your body again. What was washed off is now trying to cling back to the hair and skin on your body. The temperature shifts slowly enough not to alert your senses, but even when the water drifts completely, the difference doesn't make you want to leave. You are comfortable, and although the temperature is different, you have settled for being where you are and in your condition because to trouble the water would be more trouble than sitting. You will accept evil if that means you don't have to fight as hard for good.

But not all water is suitable for what you are seeking to do. If you need to sanitize, you cannot do that in cold water–not even in warm water. If you want to be refreshed, cold water will wake your body up. If you seek comfort, peace, or a gentle embrace, warm water may bring your body to relax. But you don't need to be lulled to sleep now! You need to be quickened, and reminded, that you have a purpose on earth!

I know that if your body is aching, you want to be in hot water, preferably with Epsom salt to relax your muscles. The Father revealed to us that He would rather we be hot or cold but not luke warm (Revelation 3:16). Are you hot or cold? Or are you sitting in stale water that is neither hot nor cold? It's not what you want or what you planned for? The water is luke warm, merely comfortable, but not because it is hitting the spot but you are too unmotivated to move.

Too unmotivated to pray, to dream, to see life beyond where you are. They say the enemy to great is good. What if the enemy's target is okay? Are you doing okay today? Is your fine, great, genuine, or another masquerade? Are you hiding from the truth that things could be better, and right now, you are coasting?

When we are stuck, we need to remember we are not alone. You are not in the world by yourself, there is a God in Heaven and people around you who can help! In Ecclesiastes 4:9-10,12, we learn the foundation for why two are better than one. "Two are better than one because they have a good return for their labor." If you feel like things are going off the mark, you may need to tap in a friend, business partner, or Yah to help fill in the gaps!

We need His guidance to help us to write the vision and make it plan so that others can also grab the vision, and run with us (Habakkuk 2:2). "And the Lord answered me and said: "Write the vision and make it plain upon tablets, that he may run that readeth it." Your dream has to be BIG enough to include other people and not just you or you and your family. The vision God has for you is to impact the Kingdom of God and the world.

Our job as believers is to bring the Kingdom of God here on earth! "Your kingdom come. Your will be done, On earth as it is in heaven (Matthew 6:10)." Your mission in life is bigger than you think. Sometimes, aren't we guilty of thinking we are too small to make a difference? Too small to impact the world or not significant enough to do something great?

I am sure people thought that of Harriet Tubman before she ran away and kept running to save hundreds of other slaves. She was a woman, bruised, abandoned by her husband, and a runaway slave with no home. Her family were all in captivity. She had a head injury when she was young, she was getting older, and her owner thought to sell her in her old age.

I am sure her vision was narrow at its inception. I don't want to be sold, was her main thought! Sometimes our big ideas start off small and they may only impact us directly. She was thinking of herself because she couldn't include anyone else. However, when she made it to the other side, she realized something. She could do this for others and encourage those around her. She saved everyone in her family–including her parents.

She was a simple woman who learned to dream big! She allowed her vision to expand beyond her personal needs and when you do the same, something that was small can become great! Her name was made permanent in American History because she allowed Yah to use her.

What gifts or talents do you have at your disposal that God can use? What did you dream about doing when you were young? What issues do you see in society that you are passionate about impacting? It doesn't have to be something grand, it can be something that you think is small.

Who would have thought picking up a basketball can impact the world? That speaking on a camera could invite you into people's homes and hearts? What about listening to people's problems and being intentional about praying for them?

It is in the simple things that you learn the power of God. In our weakness, He is made strong (2 Corinthians 2:9-11)! If you are dreaming big enough, you will need Yah and the help of others! He did not make us to be lone rangers, but with wise counsel dreams are established (Proverbs 15:22-23).

As a business owner, author, publisher, content provider, and minister, I am constantly leaning on other people and resources to help me achieve my purpose. If I need to write and publish a book, I use programs, software, and my process to get it done. Although I don't use AI to write any of my books, I do write using software like Word. I do have to understand equipment and distribution platforms. I have to have a website and know how to work my CRM and other associated services to help this business take root.

As an author, coach, business owner, or professional, you will need elements to help your business and career work. You will need a website, a CRM (client management system), social media, marketing, people to endorse you, to be organized, and so much more. I published Turn Key Solution because I realized all the things I needed to do to start a business, I could share and help others.

I have started four businesses for myself, and

working them takes a learning curve. You don't know what people will want or want to buy from you. Sometimes, what we think and how people respond are different. Don't allow this to cloud your hope and vision for the future. I know there were too many times when I questioned whether I had what I needed to win in business as an author, book publisher, and store owner.

Yes, I am still learning, but I have experience building under my belt that helps me to better coach other business owners. Even my failures have proven helpful for what I will not do. That information I share with others in the KLE Business Concierge, where we provide CRM service support and creation, new business services, website/landing page, email campaigns, workflows for automation, and more I pull from my experiences that include success and failure. This was one of the best ideas I have had, to use my experiences to help others, because I've learned that my value is linked to my purpose. I want to be a solution!

When it comes to publishing books, e-books, and audio books, I have the same goal: to help others make this process easy. When I wrote and published the book and program Write Anything Easily (WAE Process), I knew this would meet the needs of many new authors. Writing and publishing your book is not a hard process, but it is a process.

I wanted to help authors know what to do and see the value in their experience. We are all unique and gifted with something from Yah. You are already special. You are already like God. People try to sell you things based on what you perceive you don't have. The enemy got Adam and Eve to believe they were not like God in the Garden. They both believed the lie, and they ate from the Tree of Good and Evil.

This was a trick to rob humanity of its dominion, power, and connection with Yah. In the disobedience of Adam and Eve, everything associated with them also had to bear the consequences of their actions. Through Adam, men sinned all, but with the second Adam, we have mercy and grace (Romans 5:12).

We cannot afford to be ignorant of our enemies' devices and fall for this old trick of not being enough. What we don't know, what we cannot believe, can rob us of what could be. One of the greatest errors of Adam and Eve was their mistaken belief that knowledge was equal to wisdom. That false power blinds you to the truth: You cannot do everything by yourself.

Some good news, if you have identified that you are in a block in life. You are stagnant. Your worship is luke warm and your progress is mediocre. It is not about the results but your faith, your belief, your commitment, and your ability to dream and see past the physical into the spiritual. What we do is part of the process, but how we think and feel is important.

Have you noticed that repetition is heavily present in the Bible? How many times do you need to hear you win before you remember you are a winner? We may hear the Father telling us no to this or yes to that. Like children, we may need to hear the same things until we get it.

When we think we are getting away from trouble, He sees all. So what are we really doing? Daring to dream or leaning on our own understanding, talents, and ideas to determine our future? Rely upon the Word to help expand your vision.

You could have been fed a lie thinking you are not already set. That you need this great deal to have a transfer of wealth. What you think you don't have is the enemy's trick. The real numbers are not on the screen; the real thing is you. You are the system, the currency, the power. With all the power a fallen angel may have, principality, they need humanity to function on earth–they need you!

They need your essence and image of God to work their plans. Have you heard the joke about people trying to create their own humans without God's help? He invites them to try, and when man picks up the dirt to add other things to it, Yah says, "You can't use my dirt."

I always thought this joke was clever and fitting to describe humanity, the great fall, and the conditions for how we live. We want to achieve great things, thinking we don't need Yah, but our breath comes from Him. Your talents came from Him, too. Every good thing comes from Yah (James 1:17)! So who or what has come and bewitched us to believe we can't dream? You are more than a conqueror, but how many of us think we are not (Romans 8:31-39)?

The Father loves you and He cares about you.

He keeps everything and knows the number of hairs on your head. We may feel that God doesn't care or know us, but He knows your heart and what you hope for. He searches your heart, and sifts what is inside. If it is pain, trouble, fear, anxiety, hope, trust, or peace. As a man thinks so is he (Proverbs 23:7), but also what if there be good or bad in your heart, that is what you bring to others (Luke 6:45).

So are you thinking about your dream? My people perish because of a lack of knowledge. The things we don't know–or I dare say we don't believe. Dark knowledge is not wisdom; we need wisdom. Dark knowledge brought the flood.

We should know better now. We should seek righteous wisdom and not think we have to go left to go right. We need to know the enemy's devices (2 Corinthians 2:11). He comes to lie, steal, kill, and destroy (John 10:10). What has he killed in you? How has he blocked your imagination?

Influence your mind, will, and emotions, and release your soul to believe again. Your enemy cannot take your dreams, but you have to choose to give them up. What are you thinking on? Desiring? Putting yourself subject to? The enemy uses pain; the Father gives you things that are lovely, good, and He says think on good things (Philippians 4:8).

Why? To keep you hopeful. Operating out of pain and fear will have you run a mist. You will not be running from poverty but will end up poor anyhow. You can be poor in many ways, not just financially. Health, hope, time, and relationships all can point to suffering. You have to be open to the father changing your direction or expanding it.

You have to trust that His ways are greater than yours. Don't rely only on your thoughts feelings and reality. Are you your own god? But you can't be, there is only one true God. We are like God, but never can be God (Psalm 82:6). We cannot rise above Him (John 13:16). So stay hopeful.

Lean on the Word, speak scriptures that can help you. Keep good friends who speak life about your situation. You need this. This is a requirement and not a suggestion. You need to know His voice. Harriet needed to hear the Voice of Yah to direct others to freedom.

We have to make His ways our ways, like Ruth. She said she would follow what she needed to follow the God of Naomi. When we are in trouble, what are you willing to do? Sometimes, we say things don't take all of that–but if it did, would you do it?

If writing your book meant spending nights writing with no one to give you applause? If starting your business meant making calls where people said "no" or ignored you. If you had to get out there and talk to strangers, make posts, generate articles, build a website, or hire a team of people, would you do it? Would the cost be alright because your vision is big enough to pay for it?

Would your faith be big enough to keep you invested and believing as you go through the low periods? Are you willing to deny yourself or allow God to disrupt your plans so that He can give you a bigger dream? Do you want to marvel at how powerful Yah is? I wanted to see Him show up, and when my faith was too weak, He created an atmosphere where I could not hide.

He took the comfort from me. When we are comfortable, we don't hope or think for something. We are content. We stop looking for a miracle, for something more; we are content with what we have. We are also limiting God. When we operate off what we know, like 2 plus 2 is four, we know if I put this in I will get this out. There is no faith. In faith, we can put in two hours, and the outcome can vary. It can feel like zero, multiplied by unforeseen numbers, and open the door for the impossible.

Dreaming allows us to release our imagination. One thing I love about children is that they are not scared to believe. They are not afraid of their imagination and put no limits on it. They can see anything as being true. I remember my son, Ayden, asked me about the moon. He said, "Mom, what happened to the rest of the moon? I said, "Oh, when it has a party going on, it plays with the lights. It turns them off and on so only parts of the Moon shows." He said, "Really?"

I replied, "No, Son. I am just joking."

"But Mom, that would be so cool if that were true."

"We should write a book on that, Ayden. I think it would make a great story, and we can talk about the many shapes of the moon. And about the Moon dancing." This is how some of my books have come into being. Questions answered, nothing too deep. Just common conversation and living on purpose.

I get the most ideas being in position. Going to church, I hear God speak to me all the time about a new title, book, idea, or thoughts to share. I write them down and circle back to them later on. What are the areas in which you find that God speaks to you? When I pray I get all kinds of things that I pray to remember when I am done praying. Sometimes, I do, and sometimes, unfortunately, I don't remember. But I believe they will come back at the right time.

Your imagination and how you can make room for God in your average, regular life helps make room for miracles. You don't need magic; you need an active imagination and the heart of a child to dream Big! You are a child of God! There is nothing He cannot or will not do for you. Dare to Dream Big!

When you can see the forest beyond the trees and can calculate all the details, that is not Yah. When we take God by the Hand, we don't always see the end. Because we cannot see, it means we have to lean on His eyes. We have to trust His Hand and His word to carry us through. If you are at a block in life, that is a good place.

That means you are in a valley to decide if you will dare to dream big with God or walk in limitation to have what you can control out of a temporary circumstance. Nothing lasts forever. Our choices create the doors that can open to us next. We can be the reason we go nowhere or everywhere.

The world is your oyster, and you can achieve anything you set your mind to. Anything you can believe for. Anything you can have faith for. Anything you are willing to work for. You are more than a conqueror. Dare to Dream Big and believe!

Thinking Points!

A. Are you leaning on your own strength and giving excuses for why you don't pray?
B. Have you limited the power of Yah in your life, limiting His will to bless and Save you?
C. Do you trust the direction of God and believe everything is working to your good?
D. What is stopping you from taking the limits off what you can believe God for?

Now, I want you to do the Self Check-In to *Embrace Your Crown*!

I. Let's Check You In!
A. Situation
1. What is keeping you from dreaming again--believing?
B. Change
1. Do you need to change how you see God and if you see Him as a vital key to change your life?
C. Endurance
1. Focus on a miracle you need from Yah today. But I also want to challenge you to make a journal entry for what He is doing without you asking?
D. Persevere
1. As you expand your belief, you will also stretch your faith, be-

lief, and imagination. Don't feel foolish as you dream again and think on the impossible. Persevere!

E. Acknowledgments

1. Yes, all things are not for building a healthy imagination. God will not give you something that is not yours--we are not praying for people or things that are not ours, but for what God purposed for your life to make its way to you!

F. Re-Purpose

1. Spend this time remembering how good the Father has been to you. Take courage in the simple things to help build the bridge to believe for something that takes greater faith. The Father wants you to taste His good work and know He is good (Psalm 34:8). He can make you lighter so you can dream again.

G. Help?

1. If an aspect of this chapter was difficult and you want to talk about where you are, please do. Be encouraged; you are not alone. We have free and paid resources to help you work through this series. Skilled

coaches, therapists, and speakers are here to help.

Sometimes, we get stuck in a process or want to discover more about what makes us or has made us who we are. Do not feel like you can't linger on a thinking point, question, or chapter. If you need help throughout this book at any point, I want you to contact me and my team. We are a network of coaches, counselors, and prayer warriors ready to help you Embrace Your Crown, connect the dots, and go from where you are to where you are born to go.

H.	*Embrace Your Crown* Affirmations: Let's make some declarations!
1.	I am where I am but I don't have to remain here.
2.	My life is being shaped by my thoughts and I will continue to stretch my thoughts to embrace my dreams.
3.	I can see a future that has my dreams coming true.
4.	I am happy today in the journey, and I am believing that every step I take is bringing me closer to having what God

	wants for me.
5.	What is for me is for me!
6.	I am not ashamed to dream again and have hope again.
7.	I will not be my own god but trust that God's ways are higher than mine.
8.	I will keep my eyes on Yashua (Jesus) as I move forward in life.
9.	I will not jeopardize my future to save someone else but will help through obedience in Christ.
10.	I am ready to *Embrace My Crown*! Embracing who I am and who I was born to become!
11.	I am ready to TRANSFORM and Go BEYOND Change!

KICK NEGATIVITY

No More Doubt

"And the Lord answered me, and said, Write the vision, and make it plain upon tables, that he may run that readeth it." Habakkuk 2:2

The ingredient we all need to live a life of miracles and accomplish the impossible is faith! Having faith is to believe. Faith produces hope, and we need hope to build a strong belief that moves action. You need faith, fueled by belief that leads to hope, to actually make the impossible happen.

We must believe, like how children do in tv shows and movies, to change our world. We have to pursue what we believe for or else it will not happen. When we build a reputation of living by faith, long after we are dead, we can still have a legacy powered by faith and hope.

As with anything in life, everything starts with what you believe and are willing to work for. James said I will show you my faith not only by my words and prayers but also by my works (James 2:18). When we dare to dream, we are going to be moved by an area that ideally we are passionate about. It doesn't have to be major, and your action doesn't have to be grand, but you need a key ingredient: compassion.

The Good Creator started earth and brought His Son down to help man because He had compassion on us (Psalm 103:13). Furthermore, for those who fear God, He says He will have compassion on them. While we were still sinners, the Word had compassion on us and died for our sins (Romans 5:8). Compassion with no action is not compassion at all, I once heard from Pastor Dr. W. Michael Turner. When he said it, I knew I would never forget it.

There's a link to compassion and gratitude and how they both impact our lives. When we are compassionate, it will prompt our hearts to be open to share and give what people may not deserve, but God wants to use us to show His goodness. Having a soft heart that can move you to action and creates the desire to care about someone or something is powerful. This driving force helps to generate a strong "why" for how come you will work without pay. Why you will keep believing though the prosperity is slow in its manifestation, it will also keep your hope alive when you think about quitting.

Quitting is a thought that comes to us all, so don't think it is only you who ever wanted to quit.

There were many nights that I remember planning to quit or speaking it aloud out of frustration. I didn't make any moves on it affirmatively, but the words did create a lackluster sense of motivation. I wasn't moving full speed ahead anymore but taking things a day at a time when I had time.

I was losing focus on the why, or perhaps I wasn't as honest about the why. If you want to do something to pay the bills, and money is the motivation, that might not be enough to keep you going if the money doesn't come. If your heart is not fully engaged in what you want to do, a glimpse of negativity can completely derail your plans. When things tarry or don't happen, it can make you self-sabotage and speak negatively about your progress and your vision.

When you recast your vision through a negative lens, it adds so much more pressure. You are not working from a light heart, a yoke that is easy, and a burden that is light. Now, you are weighed down with the cares of this life or the disappointment of your lack of progress. I am not suggesting that you should not have goals to accomplish and that money should not be an aspect of that goal; however, I don't advise that being the sole most important goal.

The love of money is the root of all evil (1 Timothy 6:10). When we are driven by money and base our success and failure solely on that, we can cut down our progress and discourage our journey. If the Messiah based His success on how much money He made on earth by speaking and traveling the circuit of countries hand-picked by Yah, many would consider Him a failure.

He wasn't rich. He worked a job, and He had to raise an offering to afford to feed people. He was not living off of His wealth and authority to call anything down from heaven in an instant–including angels (Matthew 26:53). He worked and toiled with man and the earth the same as us.

He experienced the emotions we have all felt when we have felt alone, abandoned, hurt, and in pain (1 Peter 2:24). There was not one thing on earth that He didn't experience in the 33 years He was on earth (Luke 34:23). He had to be sure to remain in alignment with the Will of God even when that meant Him doing what He by nature would not have elected to do. If the cup He had to drink could be removed from Him, He wanted that, but not by His will but by the Father's Will (Luke 22:42-44).

The Messiah never once questioned or doubted the Command of Yah. He knew His assignment and intended to do that despite whatever problems may come His way. He was content to follow the Word of God because His heart was convinced and set on doing the will of the Father.

The Messiah was fixed on staying true to God, but what makes us doubt? The world may not believe in anything, that there is a God, or that people are either bad or good. Some people choose to make up what they believe out of thin air and seek to convince humanity to agree.

As believers, however, when we doubt, we are

not only questioning our thoughts but also the power of the Word. We are, in essence, questioning whether the Word works. But what would make us side with doubt over faith? What would be so convincing that we would jump on the bandwagon of negativity instead of being hopeful?

I think I know. Have you ever prayed for something that didn't happen? Yes, you can ask for simple things like purses, parking spaces, an additional five minutes to get to work, etc.

If those prayers don't happen, they are not as big of a deal as if you prayed for a baby and it didn't come. A husband or wife who never appeared. Or if you are going through hardship with sickness, disease, or financial issues and a positive result doesn't ensue. If you ever prayed for someone to stay alive and they died, it can be one of the hardest things to accept and to keep from making your thoughts negative.

We think yes, Yah gave me a house, food and some of the things I asked for. He is good, but He isn't really all powerful. We limit Him based on what He doesn't do. We can't say He doesn't work or doesn't hear our prayers, but we limit Him when we believe He is not all-powerful.

Believing a lie or believing a statement contrary to the truth will lead you down a path of negativity and doubt. We overcome by the hearing of each other testimony (Revelation 12:11). The whole Bible is full of testimonies, so we cannot say we don't see it.

Kick Negativity - Embrace Your Crown

But we try to put limiters on how He works for us. We start to doubt the things He said to us and about us. If you don't know how to hear from God, I didn't at one point, you can be tempted to go to prophets and others to psychics. We can be entangled in the process of finding God and miss Him completely.

How can we miss a Big God? Is it that we want to know, or do we want what we know to change? Sometimes, we can hear and say that what we heard was the devil because we don't like what He said. We can plead for mercy like how Hezekiah pleaded when Yah said something He didn't like (Isaiah 38:1-5).

We need to go to Him and not go away from Him when we are driven to embrace negativity and not hope. Saul went to a witch because the heavens were shut out from Him (1 Samuel 28:3-25). When God is far away, and we are desperate, we can tap the shoulder of people we know mean us no good to gain comfort if we believe God is far off.

What do you do when Yah is far off? There is a song I love, and it speaks so perfectly to how believers can kick negativity in the butt. Marvin Sapp has this song, "Praise Him In Advance." I love the song because of the lyrics. He says we are to praise Him in advance because our praises will confuse the enemy! In 2 Chronicles 20:21, "King Jehoshaphat had his army sing praises to God before a battle, reminding them that the battle belonged to God."

SCAN THE QR TO

LISTEN: MARVIN SAPP
"PRAISE HIM IN ADVANCE"

To circle a building praising God and entrusting your heart toward worship would be sufficient to have giant and strong walls come tumbling down. It had me so excited when I started looking at how I praised Yah. It clicked in my heart that if I wanted to get out of my funk, I had to learn to worship God when I liked what He did or if I didn't. When we can learn to praise Him in advance or in spite of the challenge, that is when we activate a new level of faith! A new level of power!

We all can love someone when the getting is good, as they say. It takes more to stay with someone when the rain, the hail, the drought, the lightning, and all hell breaks loose! Your love and belief have to be strong, or you will not survive. Romans 4:20 records, "He staggered not at the promise of God through unbelief; but was STRONG IN FAITH, GIVING GLORY TO GOD."

If you are stuck spewing negative words about yourself, your progress, or someone else, you can change things by adopting a heart of gratitude. When we give God the glory, we give Him our burdens. We lay our burdens down and leave them there. He says to His children to cast their burdens on Him because He cares about them (1 Peter 5:7). You are not casting your cares on Him if your problems blind you and shut you off from being grateful for what you already have.

Having a spirit of gratitude will get you far with anyone, but especially with God. It is a virtue handpicked by Him that keeps us from nagging (being negative) and complaining. If your eyes are too focused on your problems, you will not believe for what God is doing for you. He said that He will make all things work to the good of those who love Him and are called according to His purpose (Romans 8:28). Do you believe that ALL things work to your good? If they are working to your good, what is there to be negative about?

When we are absorbed by problems, we shut ourselves out of seeing God's goodness. Yah is Good, and He is a strong refuge for those who TRUST in Him (Nahum 1:7). Are you trusting God? Does your negative self-talk and the way you communicate about life, yourself, people, and circumstances confirm that you trust Yah or that you have limited His goodness?

We have all heard the fun slogans about why gratitude is important, but we will not honestly realize its importance until we make it personal. I remember when I had lost my apartment and my car, and I was sleeping on my sister's floor because she was kind enough to allow me to do that. I never forgot those days and the time it felt like I had nothing.

I was rolled up in a blanket with my daughters, and I knew the life I wanted to provide for them.

I couldn't get to that mark if I started harping on the negative. When we look at the negative, it can easily disguise itself as the truth. Yet, it wasn't the truth about my situation but the facts of my situation. Facts can change when the truth is revealed. We can see clearer when all the cards are on the table, and distractions are gone.

Laying on the floor without the comfort of the bed, the temperature I preferred, and the surety I had before reminded me of something I had quickly forgotten. No matter where I go and what happens in my life, I knew that God hadn't left me. I had to be reminded in that moment as I laid on the floor that He was working this out for my good!

I was thinking about why God would have to take everything away from me. Then it occurred to me I stopped listening. I wanted a relationship with my youngest daughter's father to work out. Every time I tried to get closer to making things work with him, I saw my life get knocked down a notch. When I had more, the knocks didn't hurt or could go unnoticed, but when I didn't have much left, each blow I felt, and I rested in gratitude for His mercy to bring me here; although I was saddened it took all of this.

We need to turn our hearts and minds to Him, to His Word, to know our way. If we lean on our own understanding, we might think all the wrong things and start to speak negatively about something He wants us to do. It isn't about the Word not working, but if we are in a position of obedience to go to the next level in our purpose.

Are you responding to the Word of God? Do you allow Him to pursue and fill you? Is He trying to reveal something to you?

Yah can talk in a soft voice, but He can also use people to speak for Him. For me it took my apartment complex evicting me and the repo man taking my car. For some of us, it is police officers, spirits, and other things the Father permits to show us something about ourselves. Situations can be used as a means for God to reach us.

Does the Father have to disrupt your life to contact you? Can He disrupt your life, and you believe it is for your good? When we learn to trust God, we can accept whatever the direction He pushes us into. God uses unconventional means at times to reach us, doesn't He?

Like in the case of 1 Kings 22:21-23 when He sent a lying spirit. Anyone and anything is a vessel in the Hands of God for His use. This is what makes Him sovereign. He says He can have your enemies bless you (Deuteronomy 28:7-9)!

What do you do with a God who has all access? What can anyone do to stop the plans He has for you, your business, family, finances, and life? However, if we doubt the word He has spoken concerning us, we are like Adam and Eve, who gave up a sure thing in Yah for something far less than He planned. Childbirth might not have needed to come with pain, and men could have made a living without years of toiling and working the ground but enjoying the world Yah created for them.

When we are in His will, there is more we can learn, see, and enjoy. In spite of the challenges of being either male or female, the Father has found a way to bring Heaven here on earth. Doubting Thomas had to touch the wounds of Christ to believe (John 20:27).

Are you so double-minded you cannot believe unless you already see what you should have hoped for? That is not faith at all if you believe only when you see it. As you mature in God, He might not oblige you in this way, and instead, this needed reassurance can make you miss out on the full plan God has for you, like Barak.

Barak didn't want to go to war unless Deborah, a judge and known prophetess of Yah, came with him to battle. She said she knew what she heard and would go with him because they were winning. The reason Barak was scarred is because they had been oppressed for twenty years brutally. He was looking at the evidence, the facts, and his fear. All these things compounded and shed doubt on his ability to trust God fully. He knew of the power of God but questioned on if Yah wanted to give them victory in this battle. He wanted confirmation.

Are you wanting confirmation that something you asked for was going to work out? Do you want someone to hold your hand through the ordeal? Do you know that Deborah told him because he didn't do what the Father told him to do, the praises would be had by a woman! In his culture, this was a big deal. He was the man meant to protect the women and children, yet it would appear that he was hiding behind a woman to win a battle promised to him.

When we align with the people we need, that is a good thing. However, when we put most of the burden on others to help our dreams work, don't be surprised if you don't get all the praise for it working out. It might be that those who have helped you the most get some of the light–like Deborah. The song about the battle included Deborah and Barak, with her being at the forefront. She was already established in life, and this incident extended her legacy.

If you need help in your life, ask for it, but don't be quick to ask someone to do something that you should do. When the Father reserves something for you, walk through the door. If you don't walk through it, don't be surprised if someone else does. The body is made up of many parts, and we all have an assignment so the body doesn't fail. Allow God to use you to the max, and trust His hand in your life.

When we doubt God's power, we doubt His ability to save and deliver. This doesn't hurt God or His plans—Deborah proves that—but it will hurt those who fail their assignments. When we don't listen to or follow God's will, it won't change His word or what He said. The Word works on its own. He will accomplish what He sets out to do.

So many of us miss the blessing that the world learns to tap into without the Source because they can believe! The President is an influential person we all would like to know. To have a relationship with someone who has influence is awesome when you can call him by name and pick up the phone, and they answer. You are connected when you have access. If you say you can get something done and you have access to the power to get it done, your words carry more weight than those without access. The same thing that is true in the natural is first true in the spirit.

How can you win if you don't have faith and hope, the currency of heaven? Your true battle for legacy and building the wealth the father wants is not carnal. Yashua said to give to Caesar what is his, but to me, what is mine (Mark 12:17). Where is your faith, belief, child-like faith that takes the Father at His word?

Riding a bike or learning to do something with the help of your Father (or mother) is what you rely on when doing something new, is it not? You expect them to hold the seat as you peddle down the street. One thing every parent knows is that they cannot always do that for you. They will have to take their hand off your progress and allow you to peddle and balance on your own. When they first let you go, you can get mad because you might feel that they have dropped you.

Elevation and maturity don't always feel good and can make us feel lonely at times. When we are suffering and going through our process, we can think of making others come with us to lessen our own fear. Barak wanted Deborah to help with his own fear and doubt. Doubt impacts not only you but all those associated with you and, most importantly, the Body of Christ.

We must all speak the same Word; this connects us. This makes the body strong. What makes the body weak is when we don't trust each other or what God has for us to do. Can you recall a time when your knee, leg, arm, foot, or hand fell asleep? Do you know how your whole body seemed to look at that body part with disappointment? Your mind knows your body part should work, but pins and needles or something has it feeling like jelly, and it is not strong.

When we do not operate in faith and trust, we weaken the body. Doubt can separate the body and make a part weak and giggly, like sleeping limbs. What was meant to be the strong tower has now been made weak through doubt, but not His power. Doubt will silence our prayers, distance our relationship with God, and have us believe how we live cannot be changed. "It is what it is," is how we grow to feel. We can grow to settle instead of believing for more.

Don't lean on your own power that can give way like dazed limbs. Choose to remember that God is not like men, and He doesn't lie (Numbers 23:19). Nothing will come to Him void (Isaiah 55:11), and Heaven and earth will pass away before something He says does not happen (Matthew 24:35). There are a lot of people dead and gone who had to believe in the promise that was far off, and they believed for it. Believe for your children, family, and the generations to come.

We won't all be here to fulfill all the promises God has given us, but we are part of the promise.

Those around us need us to believe. We have to kick out all doubt to move with certainty and pass the baton to those ahead of us. We are anchors for our family and stones in the foundation of something great. We can shift our families' trajectory and make something meaningful and great out of our lives.

We are leaking what and who we are. What we speak and how we treat others reflect how we see ourselves. Your emotional tank needs to be full of good things, hope, trust, and belief in the future. If you are in doubt and your mind is not open to God's impossibilities, then it would be up to the next person in line to do it for you. A double-minded man is unstable in all his ways (James 1:8).

Growing up like me, you likely didn't have a family who thought about life insurance. Most people in my family didn't think of having an insurance policy that I was aware of until something happened that required it. We are all quick to not see the need for something until we need it. If you are in need of insurance, an inevitably occurrence, that is when you cannot get it.

Don't think an attitude of gratitude or a heart set on good things is not necessary until all things are well. You need this heart and mindset now. You need to be emotionally stable no matter the storm or joyous occasion. You need to have a steadfast love toward God no matter the outcome of His decisions.

When my mom became an insurance agent offering whole-life policies, she taught me so much, and we both learned how important future planning is. We cannot truly prepare for the future if we wait until the hour to get ready. We need to prepare our hearts and finances to build a strategy now to welcome the future.

SCAN THE QR TO

CONNECT: YULANDA DYER
INSURANCE AGENT
(INDIANA)

I bought a life insurance policy, and I felt amazing afterward. I didn't think more about the policy after it started and didn't miss the money. Funny, I had thought to ensure everything else in my life, but my life and that of my children never was something that came to mind. I have been meaning to do it and learn more about it, but I didn't make it a priority. The things we really value, however, we make time for. We just have to clear distractions to take action.

I don't want negative thoughts and situations to stir my decisions. I realize that when I am not prepared, anything could come along and blow me away. If I hadn't built a relationship with God, a bad day could have sent me into a funk. I could start spiraling and second-guessing my actions and plans. This is a huge delay if we keep allowing doubt and negative thoughts to stifle our progress.

Nothing feels worse than realizing you are starting and stopping and must start back up again at the beginning. I wanted to clear my heart and reach a good place to take my life and family to the next level. I realized operating in doubt and believing that I wasn't good enough or didn't have enough was not how my business, career, and future was going to take flight.

Have you noticed that, too? Your future won't take care of itself, but you need to be like the ant working in times of good to store up. We are to leave an inheritance for our children and children's children. It is a good thing to be forward-thinking and not only focused on the here and now. The here and now can be screaming things that can make us feel like whatever is the loudest is the most important. This is not always the truth, however.

For some of us, we have been motivated more by negative reinforcement than by the positive. We have grown used to hearing people doubt us, so we become quick to beat them to the punch, and we think on the negative things people will say instead of the good. Perhaps we know there won't be any or so few to compliment us that we cannot consider this possibility. I want to encourage you that when you focus on the good, more good will come. Although we can overcome the negative, don't allow that to charge your future.

Allow your hope for the future to do it instead. This is clean energy that can fuel more growth at uncalculated speeds. Negative reinforcement is charged by pain; you want to release your pain so that you can be free as the Good Lord intends. He wants to set you free from chains, not use the chains to have you drag His vision forward for your life.

SCAN THE QR TO

ORDER: RELEASE PAIN
(FROM BONDAGE TO
FREEDOM)

Being a bond servant of Christ is not what a slave is on earth (1 Corinthians 7:22). I know sometimes we stall in putting out what we have because we think it is not good enough. It is not perfect; it is not like anything you have seen and could use considerable amounts of work. That may be true, but we all start somewhere. We are in process, and if we focus on being great, we might not see that we are good!

Funny, the Bible doesn't tell us to be great; it instructs us to be good and faithful (Matthew 25:23). You don't have to be great because that is the role of the Father, but we can be good (Psalm 95:3-7). Michael Todd preached a sermon and said that we don't have to be great; God is already that, and our job is to be good. We are to be like Christ, knowing the voice of our Father because His sheep knows His voice (John 10:27).

SCAN THE QR TO

LISTEN: PST. MICHAEL
TODD
"SERMON"

K. Lee

What has you believing something far beneath what He said about you? Whatever you are facing, healing from, problems that are dragging on, financial issues, marital problems, family strife, division, separation from your job, unforgiveness, personality issues, emotional trauma, distrust, anger, resentment, and anything else, God is Bigger (Isaiah 40:12, 25-31). He offers deliverance so that you can be set free to believe. We become a new creature (2 Corinthians 5:17), and we are no longer what we used to be but who He wants us to become.

You today is not everything you will grow to become. Don't beat yourself up for where you are, but kick negativity to encourage the faith you need to not only survive but thrive! Because your negativity can block miracles. Negativity and doubt can cancel miracles. Don't doubt. If you doubt, you cannot be obedient, which is why you need to learn to trust God. The power is in His Word.

Thinking Points!

A. Have you been operating from a negative mindset?

B. Did you discover that negative reenforcement is how you have been working best?

C. Do you know that people are rooting for your success and even more so, than your failure?

D. Are you leaving room for you to grow and expand pass predictable expectations?

Now, I want you to do the Self Check-In to *Embrace Your Crown*!

I. Let's Check You In!
  A. Situation
    1. All of us have been told hurtful words that we need to process how they will impact our lives?
  B. Change
    1. Whose word means the most to you? God's or someone else's? Do you feel you need to make God's opinion greater than all others in your life?
  C. Endurance
    1. It is an adjustment to shift our hearts and minds from what we were groomed to believe about ourselves to what God sees in us. In tears I have come to real-

ize what I wanted and believed for myself was way underneath what God had in store for me. Are you open to see what Yah has for you?

D. Persevere

1. I know it takes work to expand our beliefs and throw out the many things we believe about ourselves. But when we are at our lowest and most broken, God can put us back together the way He intended for us to be. It is in our brokenness that He can fuse and mend all cracks in our hearts, minds, goals, dreams, and parts we never knew were broken. Persevere and trust His process!

E. Acknowledgments

1. When we see the source of our doubt, we can confront it and decide how we want to move forward! We can make an informed choice about whether to believe a lie or take God's truth to heart.

F. Re-Purpose

1. When the enemy tells you you are not enough, respond and say, "Yes, I am!" As you continue to build up your voice to battle the thoughts that start in

your mind and seek to leak out into your actions, block them by thinking of good things.

G. Help?

1. If an aspect of this chapter was difficult and you want to talk about where you are, please do. Be encouraged; you are not alone. We have free and paid resources to help you work through this series. Skilled coaches, therapists, and speakers are here to help.

Sometimes, we get stuck in a process or want to discover more about what makes us or has made us who we are. Do not feel like you can't linger on a thinking point, question, or chapter. If you need help throughout this book at any point, I want you to contact me and my team. We are a network of coaches, counselors, and prayer warriors ready to help you Embrace Your Crown, connect the dots, and go from where you are to where you are born to go.

H. *Embrace Your Crown* Affirmations: Let's make some declarations!

1. I will allow good and healthy thoughts to manifest and take root in my life!
2. I am intentional of removing doubt by standing on faith.
3. If the enemy thinks or dares to say I cannot, I will choose to believe and say, "Yes I can!"
4. I will not think on things that make me feel small but focus on what makes me a giant and more than a conqueror.
5. Today, I believe again in the Power of God!
6. I will allow my trust in God to build my faith in Him.
7. I have taken the limits off of Yah and I see Him as all-powerful.
8. Nothing is impossible for me because I believe! I am free!
9. I am ready to *Embrace My Crown*! Embracing who I am and who I was born to become!
10. I am ready to TRANSFORM and Go BEYOND Change!

Kick Negativity - Embrace Your Crown

TAKE COURAGE

You Have To Work

"But he said, "What is impossible with man is possible with God." Luke 18:27

No matter what you do in life, it takes guts. It takes guts to be who you were born to be. It takes courage to tell others no when it could mean you are the odd man out. It can be hard to stand on your own with fingers pointed at you, but how many of us know we all have to do it?

If we are not willing to stand up for ourselves and speak up, how will others know what we are called to earth to accomplish? I know it is tempting to try to blend in and go along to get along. At times, however, this won't do. You will have to choose a side, and often, the side you choose will open or shut doors.

You cannot be on both teams who are competing against each other. You cannot be both for and against yourself, because a double-minded person is unstable in all of their ways (James 1:8)! When we are not of one opinion on a matter, it can confuse others about where we stand and expose a fickle mindset lurking in the background. It is okay not to know something and, therefore, have no opinion on the matter to voice. However, to feel a particular way and not voice your thoughts–with wisdom is an extreme disservice to yourself.

Have you heard of the saying, "A closed mouth doesn't get fed?" We close our mouths when we are silent about what we want and hope for or withhold giving gratitude for what we have. We are blocking avenues that could bless us and work for our good. We are choking out the life in our dreams because we shut ourselves down long before anyone else could.

When we speak negatively about our future and our plans, it is a "Debbie Downer " for our purpose. We need to believe in what we are called to do so that that belief can empower courage! When we believe, it is a dangerous weapon to doubters, skeptics, and haters of our progress. These people, systems, and hidden agendas love to feed off the weak in heart—those who don't challenge the systems that exist but play ball.

You will undoubtedly attract attention When you step out of the pack. First, you will get the people who say you can't do it, and you need to quit now before you are embarrassed. They will push the fear of embarrassment and play on your emotions. They will use the information to back it up, too. Saying things like, "Statistically speaking, tons of people have dreamed and didn't make it doing what you want to do. You should focus on something concrete."

This advice is not always meant to be negative but can be discouraging. I want to be clear: there are steps to achieving your goals. Everyone's road to success and what they want to achieve is different. No two people have the same set of circumstances and ambitions. You have to be open to what your process will be. Some of us will need to work a job and go up the ladder. Others can come in with education and leapfrog the process. Yet another class that has a shoe end because of networking and affiliations.

There is also truth in objections, but that doesn't mean that is the final say. I love the song by Maurette Brown Clark, "It Ain't Over." At the end of the song, she starts to minister that "God has the final say." No matter what is going on and what will oppose you, the final say is the Lord's. His plans for you are a sure thing. My question to you is, do you see His Word as a sure thing?

SCAN THE QR TO

LISTEN: MAURETTE CLARK
"IT AIN'T OVER"

When we see His Word as all-powerful, it will

allow us to believe in the impossible. It will free us to see life the way He does with no limits, and the only boundary is His will for your life. It is a great place to be to know you cannot fail. Again, a song I must share is "No Failure" by Melvin Crispell III and "He Won't Fail" by Todd Galberth. What I love about both of these songs is they say He won't bring you far to fail you now. He won't build up your hope, belief, and trust in Him to fail you. He will do anything but fail.

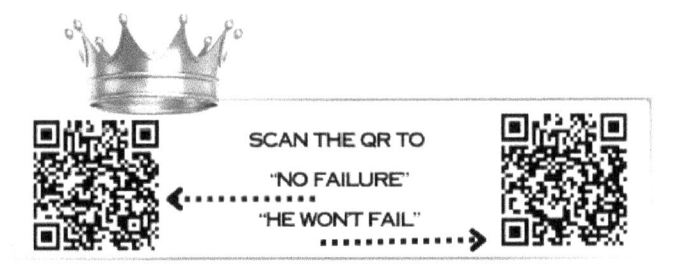

SCAN THE QR TO

"NO FAILURE" ⬅

"HE WONT FAIL" ➡

So, what must we do when we believe in the Word? We have dared to Dream–and to dream Big! No longer are we our worst critic kicking our own sand castle down, but we are speaking life over our dreams and plans. Essentially, we are making room for miracles in our lives, knowing the promises of God concerning us. So, now, what must we do when we stand here?

Have you ever been on a roller coaster ride and been at the top of a slope? You know the drop is coming, and you can do nothing to stop it. So you take courage by taking a large breath, letting out a scream, or feeling your heart drop deep into your feet. This is my thought as I hover in the air and drop several feet. I love the rides that swing around at great heights because of the view, and the motion feels excellent.

When we are used to walking and at times walking slow, it is a good morale booster to feel the movement accelerated. Being on rides like this move me faster than I can walk, and take me higher than I can jump. It is a powerful feeling but the fear of heights is real also. For some of us, we don't like heights, we don't like motion, we like being on the ground. I can empathize.

So what about water? Have you ever been to a beach and are having a wonderful time in the parts of water you are most comfortable with? For me, it is the shallow end. Yet, laughing to myself, we know there is that sneaky wave that creeps past your surveillance. Your inner sense can feel the water invisibly tapping you on the shoulder to sound your alarm of the impending crash of a wave. Although you sense it coming, nothing may prepare you for the overflow of water over your head, arms, hips, legs, and feet. Sometimes, these waves can even take us underwater!

If you are not a swimmer or a water lover, this can send fear through your body. Most people who drown drown because of panic. When we don't feel prepared, we can panic when something we have not prepared for happens. If you are not expecting a shift in life circumstances and it happens, we can sink fast. We can lose sight of the surface and feel like the pressure of the wave and the surrounding water have us helplessly flailing around to no avail. We can feel powerless and not empowered.

Do you know how to float? You have to relax. When you are ready to take your life to the next phase, you have to be willing to relax so you can be open to perceive what is happening around you. You need a clear and level head to think. If you have a busy or messy life, try cleaning up your space. I know you might feel that you are losing or wasting time, but I assure you that you are not.

When I feel overwhelmed by a project, or I get sick with a cold or something, I take it easy and rest. Your body was built to give you alerts for what it needs, but are you listening? There is a time for everything under the sun (Ecclesiastes 3:1-11). There is a time for you to prepare and a time to move!

For some of us, we don't mind going to school. We can be there forever, ever learning but not using what we have learned. We can think that being a good student will produce what we desire, but the facts point to the opposite. Many people take up majors they never use. But why? Some of us are more comfortable studying our dreams than living them because the fear of failure, the need to take courage and do it, is always the next step away. It is the dangling carrot that is inspiring but never achievable.

We can keep make excuses for why our future evades us, can't we? Oh, I didn't accomplish this goal because I didn't have the degree they had. I struck out because there was something not right in me.

How many of you know how favor works? Favor is when you get something that should have not come. The Hebrews won battles that they should not have won. People got high-ranking positions like becoming a king or queen–that they should not have received.

What was the key they used to unlock the signs, miracles, and wonders? They were willing to take courage, take God at His Word, and work the plan. They were willing to believe something so outlandish to the natural, but it was possible with God! They had to keep their eyes on Him, or they would not have survived. Is your eye on God so that you can take courage?

It is not good enough to only believe–even the demons believe and tremble from fear of Yah but don't follow Him (James 2:19). You need the extra push to work out what you believe by putting your actions in motion. You have to be willing to put work behind what you believe. For what you say you want, don't you know He will give us the desires of our hearts for those who follow His commandments (Psalm 37:4). We have to be willing to implement what we say we believe and step out on faith.

The Bible commands us to work out our soul salvation (Philippians 2:12). It takes effort. Have you had a relationship where the other person had no effort? They never contributed to plans or put up their contribution for finances, and when they arrived, they didn't even bring the fun! How much of a weight have they become for you? Are they not a dark cloud you want the sun to come out and blow away?

We can't say this because some of these people

Take Courage - Embrace Your Crown

are family members or even our spouses. What can you do when you can't leave but you have to work through the drama? You believe for it even if you are alone in your belief. Everyone will not see what you do. Some of them will not believe with you, and you must have enough power to encourage yourself in the Word like David did (1 Samuel 3:6).

If you feel heavy today, I want you to play one of the songs I mentioned in this book and dance! I know it sounds silly, but when you start to dance and put your mind on good things–things that are lovely, you will encourage your spirit. Why do you think David danced so hard to take his clothes off (2 Samuel 6:14-22)?

He wasn't stripping and trying to bring attention to himself, but he became selfless and allowed his admiration for what God had already done to move his hands, feet, hips, and shoulders. He was willing to be a sight of amusement if that's what he became, to embrace the goodness of Yah! Don't be afraid to worship God for His goodness.

Are you willing to extend your gratitude to God and allow praise breaks to enter your day? Sometimes, when I am working, I just start worshiping Yah. I start praying when something that I read touches my spirit and brings tears by the power of God. We cannot always express what we are thinking or how we feel; we just KNOW the Presence of the Almighty God has arrived.

He is not waiting on your few hours at church to enter your world. When I was writing this book,

I got stuck a few times. I never want to write something that He is not taking the lead on. If I don't feel His Presence prompting the content, I stop writing. I will push a deadline back before I put out something that doesn't have His stamp on it. Writing as Krystal doesn't have the same power as speaking with the Word and His transformational might. I write not to fill pages but to be a vessel of God to help change lives!

When you read my books I want you to feel the power of witness and for the Word of God to visit you. He has all power, I am just an ambassador of the Kingdom of Yah. When I get stuck in writing or with a client–even before I get a client, I pray. In business, the last thing you need is a trail of disappointed clients. People who do not like what they purchased or cannot use what they bought as intended.

Chargebacks are negative in the eyes of merchant processing companies and for your business's reputation. I try my best to avoid them and believe in customer service and quality work. Am I perfect? Not by far. I am a human, and I do make mistakes, but I don't want the errors to disrupt your ability to see the power of God in what I have to offer.

In your business or career, you won't fire on all cylinders all the time. Sometimes, you can have an off day, but you are still expected to perform. One moment someone has with you can shape or reshape their perception of you. I know it is not fair, but it is the real.

The Bible says to always have a reason for the hope you have in good or bad times (1 Peter 3:15).

Take Courage - Embrace Your Crown

This is easier said than done sometimes, I know, but we are to be blameless. "The Lord detests those whose hearts are perverse, but he delights in those whose ways are blameless (Proverbs 11:20)."

Nobody wants a dead relationship that lacks works to support what they say. When you are with someone who won't work to talk, be honest, helpful, or supportive, you can lose the courage to move forward for what you want. You can be tempted to settle because you cannot see beyond the trees.

I want to encourage you not to become a coward who loses the courage to move because they don't know everything. They may feel that their opposing force appears bigger and stronger. Cowards are people who don't have the power of faith. People who don't want anything that doesn't come easily enough choose a limited existence because they refuse to harness their own power and belief in themselves.

It is easy to sit on a couch and complain about other people. To see what they are doing and have an excuse for why you can't or you don't. You can make cowardice seem justified and the right solution the longer you sit. An idle mind is the devil's workshop (2 Thessalonians 3:11). When you waste your time, you are a target for cowardice and stagnation. The apostle Paul notes that people who waste their time are easily led into sin (2 Thessalonians 3:11).

Proverbs 16:27 says, "Idle hands are the devil's workshop; idle lips are his mouthpiece." Another good one is 1 Timothy 5:13: "Besides that, they learn to be idlers, going about from house to house, and not only idlers but also gossips and busybodies, saying what they should not." The Bible describes these traps for how idlers and busybodies waste time that could be used to help others. To look at what you don't have, to justify why you are not doing anything. To blame your laziness or lack of faith on someone else.

But your legacy is yours. What you do with your life and how you spend your time are up to you. If you choose not to work, you won't have when you need it. When we work and give, we are storing up treasures where the moth and thief cannot steal. Do you know why you should give?

The Bible says we should be like the ants working during harvest, storing up for drought. When we work, give, and do the right things, when we don't have enough, the reserve will come through. When we gain, it will be the power of God working to give us the power to gain wealth.

The Father will bless a cheerful giver (2 Corinthians 9:6-7). It is better to give than receive (Acts 20:35). When we give to serve others, we are planting seeds. When you do anything, the Bible tells us to do as unto the Lord (Colossians 3:23-24). When operating in your business, relationships, partnerships, or anything else, we are to see how we treat people from the lens of whether God will be happy. Is this an acceptable gift like what Abel gave or one He will hate like Cain's offering (Hebrews 11:34)?

Abel saw Yah as his source. He showed his

gratitude and trust in Him to provide. If we don't demonstrate our faith as leaders, parents, and spouses, how can we encourage others to follow us? Sometimes, we don't have relationships that demonstrate effort because we are not given effort either.

It is wrong to hold people to a standard that you don't try to live. We can know the Word and not live it. We can put yokes on people and get rid of grace and hope when they fail. When we do that, we must also point a finger to examine ourselves (2 Corinthians 3:5). "Examine yourselves, to see whether you are in the faith. Test yourselves. Or do you not realize this about yourselves, that Jesus Christ is in you? -- unless indeed you fail to meet the test!"

If you have no rest or no help, come to the One who can give you rest so you can think (Matthew 11:28). He can show you away above the obstacles and work miracles. The Father loves a good test! Job was a test and it was for His glory (Job 1:8-21). Miracles come from Yah, and He permits obstructions; humans can be used and systems.

Your success and prayers have been answered, but are they being held up like how the Prince of Persia stopped Daniel's answer to his prayer (Daniel 10:13-21)? For some of us, we pose an incredible threat to the success of our business, marriage, and relationships to the kingdom of darkness. They are praying day and night to oppose you, and our job is to pray for the will of God to overcome them!

Take courage and know that your God is bigger than all others. In our obedience, we will be rewarded (Psalm 119:2-3), and what we do in secret will be acknowledged openly (Matthew 6:4). When you work, let your light shine before others, so that they may see your good works and give glory to your Father who is in heaven (Matthew 5:16).

Search your heart for the reason you do a thing. Is it for the glory of you or to the glory of Yah? But if you do the hard work now, write now, study now, doing this and that not for the claps but to please Him, He will bless you.

He will repay all those who have given to Him. Those who pursue the Kingdom of God and His righteousness, He will add everything else unto them (Matthew 6:33). If you are in want, need, or in a drought and you feel hopeless and powerless, take courage. You need to pick up your cross (Matthew 16:24-26 and Luke 9:23), but what is that?

You have to deny yourself and lean into the promises of Yah. You need to know the Word is your Bread (Matthew 4:4). What is your Word? What is your belief? What is the word for your hope, dream, and purpose? You need to know what it is. How can you endure to the end if you don't have power (Matthew 24:13)? Unless you have a Word to help shape your courage, you will not have all the resources to help you win in life.

The world can be a dark and scary place. We are going against life circumstances, issues, principalities, and so much more. If we fall seven times, He will be there to pick us up and push us forward. He will not leave you nor forsake you (Deuteronomy

31:8). If you feel like you are failing with your book, business, purpose, family, dreams, and goals, take courage!

He is not the God of the cowards; He is for the bold, mighty, and full of faith—those who are like King David, willing to grab a slingshot and a rock. No uncircumcised Philistine is going to take what belongs to Yah and how you play a part in it (1 Samuel 17:26). When you are at war, you need to be fully convinced you have the power to win!

You need to know that there isn't a demon in hell going to stop what the Good Father is doing in and through you. No demon or devil could stop Jesus. No one could tamper with His emotions or shift His focus. Nor could they take His will when He was in jail or at the Mount praying. He didn't lose faith but took courage!

He used that time to spend with the Father. He didn't run from the day; he prayed and fasted to be ready for the hour. Take courage and do the work following to the end. Are you doing the work for your children, family, marriage, business, and, most importantly, God, or have you given up? Are you running from the vision or embracing it?

Are you losing to the kingdom of darkness because you lack power and courage? Are you robbed of your hope? Are you deflated? Do you feel like what you are doing doesn't matter? Are you so busy looking at the facts that you cannot believe for anything greater than where you are?

K. Lee

Can you not see the whole picture? Do you see ways to give God glory on your job? For how He can use you where you are to stretch you to be all He planned for you to become?

David going against Goliath was possible because Yah was his strength. You are like David when you are taken on a business and going after your goals to start something that is a challenge for you. You have to believe in something beyond what you can see. You need to be full of courage to be a trailblazer. You will make a way so that others can walk on dry land (Exodus 14:29).

Are you robbed of peace or joy today? The Father can give it back to you. He says I will give you peace and joy that surpasses all understanding (Philippians 4:7). He is the Prince of Peace (Isaiah 9:6); do you have Him? I learned to be cool with a lot or a little (Philippians 4:11-13). All of us will be challenged, so don't be deflated because of what you must endure.

Paul says, "If I might boast in what I go through like the others do to prove my value. Let me tell you what I've been through, not for me to get the glory, but so you can see my weaknesses (2 Corinthians 12:5). When we abort our mission and jump from the vessel or problem meant to fulfill our purpose, we gain nothing. Those who jumped from the slave ships, I will not judge if it was right or wrong. However, their legacy is not here today. The offspring they threw overboard is gone and resting at the bottom of the ocean. Did that work? I don't know.

I do have this question: Where would we be if the Messiah dodged the cross? Where would we be if those who have died for our freedoms chose to stop and save themselves? Would we be here now? Would we be in the promise of Dr. Martin Luther King Jr.? We all have a race to run, and we cannot dodge every droplet of rain. Some will hit us and hurt us. The Messiah couldn't run.

He lost people. His friend died, and He saw many others die. He saw people healed, living, and refreshed, but He also saw people robbing, stealing, killing, you name it. He wept (John 11:35); He cried too. Not just you. You are not alone.

It is not just you going through this. You are not the only one who needs a miracle or who needs to kick negativity. You must dare to believe if you don't know which way is up.

If you only ask for what you can do, you are not believing. Yashua (Jesus) is all that He says He is. What are you afraid of? Fear not because I am with you [Jesus](Isaiah 41:10). This isn't magic but a promise.

Please know how He feels about you and how He created humanity. He created them, male and female, and He said it was good (Genesis 5:2). We are to be good, and His greatness makes us good. Even in our falling nature, He can redeem us.

Take courage. Everything we need to transform our lives, we have it. Let's get ready to transform and go beyond change!

Thinking Points!

    A.   How do you feel about cowardice?
    B.   Do you feel encouraged reading this chapter, knowing you are not alone?
    C.   Do you believe you have everything you need to transform your life?
    D.   Whatever you need today to improve your life, be reminded that Jesus is that, too!

Now, I want you to do the Self Check-In to *Embrace Your Crown*!

  I. Let's Check You In!
    A.   Situation
    1.   Are you moving away from your goals because you are afraid to see them through?
    B.   Change
    1.   Challenge yourself to believe for something greater in your relationships, on your job, in your finances, your health, or anywhere else you need the Word to bring change in your life.
    C.   Endurance
    1.   You will never be left or abandoned. With the power of Heaven fighting your battles, how can you lose? Be full of faith, boldness, and confidence.
    D.   Persevere
    1.   With this confidence, how can

you give up now? You have come too far for the Father to fail you now. He will not fail you. Persevere and believe!

E.   Acknowledgments

1. As you work to believe, things might not change overnight. I will say they likely will not, so don't get discouraged. Know that matters of the heart, problems, and situations didn't take moments to get nasty but years. Be patient and think about the good things while waiting for your miracle. Things will turn around, and by faith, we accept they already have.

F.   Re-Purpose

1. When you get pushback from those you are trying to help, make that your golden opportunity to outshine what the devil meant for evil and turn it for God's glory. When we are good and demonstrate Christ's love to those who might reject it, we are heaping coals on the heads of our enemy (Romans 12:20). When we are good when others do us wrong, our actions call on God to intercede, and fight our battles.

G.   Help?

1.   If an aspect of this chapter was difficult and you want to talk about where you are, please do. Be encouraged; you are not alone. We have free and paid resources to help you work through this series. Skilled coaches, therapists, and speakers are here to help.

Sometimes, we get stuck in a process or want to discover more about what makes us or has made us who we are. Do not feel like you can't linger on a thinking point, question, or chapter. If you need help throughout this book at any point, I want you to contact me and my team. We are a network of coaches, counselors, and prayer warriors ready to help you Embrace Your Crown, connect the dots, and go from where you are to where you are born to go.

H.   *Embrace Your Crown* Affirmations: Let's make some declarations!
1.   I am not a coward but bold in faith and confidence.
2.   I have the power to change my life and the world around me.
3.   I will have a legacy and use my

gifts and talents to build up my children and the Kingdom of God.
4. Although I don't have everything, I do have what I need to be who I am and change my future.
5. I am full of faith believing that God is all-powerful and able to change my finances, family, health, and my spiritual and personal life.
6. I will dare to believe in the promises of God and put action behind what I believe.
7. I will leave earth empty, having done all that I was supposed to do to fulfill my purpose.
8. I know that I am not alone, and because of my relationship with God, there is nothing I fear.
9. I am no longer a runner, running away from challenges and problems. I won't provoke a fight, but I do believe I can win my battles with Christ.
10. Great is your Faithfulness, which reminds me that nothing I can believe in you cannot do, and you won't do if it is within your will for my life.
11. I am ready to *Embrace My Crown*! Embracing who I am and who I was born to become!
12. I am ready to TRANSFORM and

Go BEYOND Change! K. Lee

Believe in the Impossible Becoming Possible

"The signs of a true apostle were performed among you with utmost patience, with signs and wonders and mighty works." 2 Corinthians 12:12

If you are ready to believe in the impossible becoming possible, you need a word for it. This whole book is about power. You need the presence of God to have power. Why do you think He says that His name is I AM?

The Most High is wherever His Word is. I am that I am. So, if you need Him to enter your life, you need to be familiar with His Word by reading, studying, and praying. You need to spend time with Him to learn what all He can become for you. If you want to Transform and Go Beyond Change, you need to change your relationship with the Word.

The Word needs to be the foundation of your life for how you live, how you see things, and what you want in life. The Word should also form the foundation for what you believe you need to be and become. The Word has to be fashioned in you.

This desire has to be more important than your feelings, mind, and will. I think your commitment needs to be confessed daily. There is something every day for us to work on. We need to ask Yah to search us and renew in us a clean heart and right spirit.

We are doing this active work because much needs to change. It is not a one-and-done, but a transformation–a soul transformation that we pursue. Clean our hearts, Father, we ask, but why? Why do we need to be cleaned if we are already good? Simple: there is work within us that we must complete to share with the world and give to the Kingdom of God.

The great work He starts, He will finish it. He is big, great, powerful, and all-knowing. He is not backing up. He will be indebted to no man. If He says it, it's settled. Take courage and believe you are in the most powerful and loving hands in all the worlds.

The Word is the way to make the impossible possible. He makes it possible through Christ. The living Word is not dead. Not a dead idle or figure nailed to a cross. The Word rose, taking the keys from hell, death, and the grave. What are you afraid of?

Greater works are you able to do because He says He sits at the right hand of the Father (Hebrews 10:12-13). Do you believe that? Before there was anything, the Word was. Everything that is or will be was through Him.

Who or what do you believe? In the Rock of Ages or your opinions? Another gospel, your limited understanding? I want to encourage you to transform your life. I put before you life and death if you don't know what to choose, choose life, Yah tells us in the Bible (Deuteronomy 30:19).

Think on things that are pure and good. Be in the light. Choose to be a light bearer who shows God's goodness. He will bring miracles, signs, and wonders to those working for Him.

Trust produces Transformation. Believe in the Impossible becoming Possible! What was impossible before is now possible through Christ Yashua, your Lord and Savior! Hope produces endurance, so remain hopeful no matter what. Transform and Go Beyond Change.

Let's Transform and Go Beyond Change! Until the next book, where we Sharpen your focus, shalom, shalom, and bye-bye for now.

Transform Go Beyond Change- Embrace Your Crown

ABOUT THE AUTHOR

About Author

"God blesses those who work for peace, for they will be called the children of God." Matthew 5:9

Krystal Lee is proud to have authored this book and accompanying course to better the lives of readers. She has a heart to help people in their deepest times of need. She writes because she believes there is power in sharing stories and life accounts, that others can benefit and learn from. Sharing is caring, so she shares stories, ideas, and resources to better the lives of her readers.

In addition, Dr. Lee has authored over 35 books across twelve or more genres (adult, children, youth fiction, self-help, spiritual growth, novels, and more), in addition to ghostwriting and editing more than 20 published works. She has launched coaching programs, web courses, and helped in the formulation of many startup

About the Author - Embrace Your Crown

companies. Her specialty lies in aiding coaches, creatives, and service-based companies in defining their message, brand, unique selling point, client avatar, and generating a sales cycle and structure for her clients.

Empowering individuals is at the core of her work, and she is driven by her passion to continue writing. In addition to being an author, Krystal Lee is a business owner of multiple companies, a consultant, an ordained chaplain, and a speaker.

CONNECT

Dr. Krystal Lee

For more information about Dr. Krystal Lee scan the QR. To engage with the Coaching series and Monthly Meet up Group for Embrace Your Crown First Sundays at 4pm, please use the QR or visit InviteEyc.com and EmbraceYourCrown.com

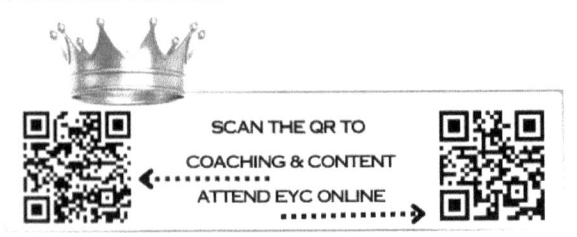

SCAN THE QR TO
COACHING & CONTENT
ATTEND EYC ONLINE

RESOURCES

Congratulations!

Great job on completing the second book in a three part series! Your decision to engage and read to the very end is an accomplishment that you should celebrate. I have gifts for you and resources that I believe will help you.

Starting my businesses, same as writing every book and publishing, so far 32, took a team and a process. If you are looking to take a journey into your own business or write and publish a book of any kind, I want to share a resource with you: WAE Process and KLE Publishing. If you want to start a business, KLE Business Concierge has been extremely helpful. More details down below.

Lastly, if you want to pick up your next book I wanted to give you a short list of some good books from

Resources - Embrace Your Crown

several genres that I can recommend from my collection. Scan QR or order at AuthorKLee.com

Spiritual Growth:
Bless the Works of My Hands 21-Day Devotional
Release Pain (40 Day Devotional)
The Embrace Your Crown Series (3 books!)
- Open 7 Gates to Find and Overcome Heartbreak
- Open 5 Gates to Overcome Unbelief
- Open 3 Gates to Sharpen Your Focus

Christian Fiction (Novels that Inspire)
Leaking
The Gray Space
The Monster
We Expect Drip, Not the Downpour
The Alone But Never Lonely Series

Children's Books
Put Your Helmet On
The Weight of the Elephant
Loves You
Samantha's Greatest Gift
The Lesson Series for Youth and Teens (10 books!)

Books for Him (Husbands/Sons)
The Biggest Mistake Can Cost You Everything
Rise and Fall of King Saul
The Ecstasy
Over the Fact

Starting a Business: Turn Key Solution: (Series)
- Go From Dreaming to Paid
- Nail Your Sales Goals: Books & Services

Writing & Publishing Your Book Easily! (Series)
- Write Anything Easily (Books & E-Books)
- Creating the Perfect Story (Novels, Scriptwriting, Audio books)

K. Lee

If you are looking to launch a business, write and publish a book, or need help automating and expanding your business, I can not say enough about Krystal Lee Enterprises (KLE) services to help handle your endeavors.

Coaching Services: Lee and her Team help people find their purpose and live on purpose.

Writing and Publishing Department: Writing services for Businesses, Websites, Documents, Books/E-books, Production Scripts, and Plays.

The Business Concierge: Offers Small and New Business Services that include Message and Brand development, Client Demographics, Sales Structure and Sales Cycle Creation. Along with Social Media and Website support, and CRM creation and management services.

Production: This department supports Film, Video, TV, Plays, Podcasts for scripting, recording, distribution, and more.

If you are ready to get started with any of these services, KLE would like to give you a special promotional offer of 10% off your entire order when you use the QR code to fill out the short survey. Your promo can be applied to books, courses, and services offered by KLE.

770-240-0089 EXT. 0
info@KrystalLeeEnterprises.com

**AuthorKLee.com
Creator of *WAE Process***

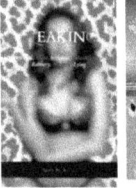

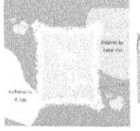

SCAN ME

Call or Text:
770-240-0089 Press Extension 1
Web: KLEpub.com
Email Services@klepub.com

It's time to start and finish   **YOUR Story**!

KLE Publishing specializes in helping people become authors. In as little as 15 to 90 days, we can help you develop your books and e-books and publish to 39,000 outlets! We also offer audiobook services.

Write, Edit, Format, Publish
We can help from
Start to Finish.

Explore and learn more about published authors affiliated with KLE.

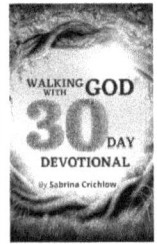

KLEPub.com